NAVEL – GAZING

(The Art of Psychic Belly Button Reading)

Written & Copyright 2013 – All Legal Rights Reserved

Dr. Jonathan Royle

www.psychicbellybuttonreading.com

www.psychicbellybuttonreading.co.uk

www.magicalguru.com

www.ultimatehypnosiscourse.com

www.elitehypnosisbootcamp.com

www.twitter.com/roylehypnotist

www.facebook.com/jonathan.royle

DEDICATION

This book entitled

"Navel - Gazing"

And Subtitled:

"The Art of Psychic Belly Button Reading"

Written by

Dr. Jonathan Royle

is dedicated to:

My Dad (who taught me the ropes in show-business)

And

My Mum (who wrote the following poem)

The 13th of August '75
Was the happiest day that I've had
When you came screaming into the world
The pain suddenly seemed not so bad.

The years flew by so quickly
And at 4 you started school.
That first day I was so upset
But you stayed oh, so cool.

Until it came to lunchtime
And then the tears came fast
you wanted to stay for your dinner!
Home for lunch? That day was the last.

Remember the Christmas production?
You were one of the Billy Goats Gruff.
And watching you up there I felt so proud
But for you it wasn't enough.

You wanted to go on performing
and went with your Dad as a Clown.
You stole the show from the TV chimps
When you appeared in New Brighton town

Then again to Gandey's Circus
With your Dad you once more set off.
But you played in a place where you shouldn't
And a Puma pulled your ear off.

But it didn't stop you performing
Off to hospital for treatment and pad,
An injection and sweet – then a quick change
And back in the ring with your Dad.

We moved to a house in Ainsworth
You didn't like it much there.
But at church you sang a solo
And at home showed your magical flair.

Then we moved back to Heywood
At one time we'd nearly a zoo
With rabbits (and babies) and pigeons
And then there was Smokey too.

No time and you were eleven
And off to Siddal Moor.
I was at work, so each morning
You saw me off at the door.

Then bad news we lost Granddad Nation.
I couldn't be here for you then.
He left us so many good memories
Don't you wish we could live them again?

You carried on with your magic,
Fire-eating and juggling too.
Then came the tarot and hypnotism
Is there anything you can't do?

Well your childhood has gone so quickly
We've seen all the illnesses through.
Measles and Mumps, German Measles
And a bad case of Chickenpox too.

Now today you're 18 and an adult
You've the rest of your life ahead
But I'll always remember your years as a child
When I'd watch you asleep in bed

And so, to the future you're looking.
I wish you Good Luck and Success,
Good Health, Good Friends and a long life,
I hope filled with happiness.

But I'll always be there if you need me.
You'll always have somewhere to come.
And there'll always be someone who loves you
While I'm on this earth – your Mum!!

COPYRIGHT NOTICE

The entire contents of "Navel Gazing" **(Subtitled: The Art of Psychic Belly Button Reading)** is strictly copyright in every way, shape and form! No part of this publication may be reproduced and/or transmitted in any conceivable existing form or by way of any other form of communication which may be invented in the future whether written, audio, filmed, mechanical, computer data, internet or otherwise without the prior express written permission of both the author Alex William Smith (Jonathan Royle) and also the publishers. This copyright does not exclude the use of short extracts for use in reviews of this book.

© 2013 Alex William Smith (Dr. Jonathan Royle)

CHAPTER ONE

WHY BELLY BUTTON READING?

The Key Reason that my approach of Psychic Belly Button Reading is so Successful is, I believe because it is very personal to the person you are doing the reading for, after all what could be more personal and intimate than studying an area of their own body?

Secondly the fact that Belly Buttons are strange and unusual sounding things and have a very interesting background as detailed within this chapter makes the idea of Psychic Belly Button Reading seem all that more fun & credible.

In otherwords it seems so wacky and bizarre that it must be true as surely you wouldn't try and fool somebody with something as daft as this if it wasn't real would you?

That's the state of mind people will be in when you start doing Psychic Belly Button Readings for them, which is ideal as it means they are more open minded and relaxed and that will help you to tune into their energies more easily.

Oh and of course the Human Navel can also be used as a focus of concentration as it is in Yoga and Meditation which is often referred to as ""Navel Gazing", however if you read my other book "The Encyclopedia of Hypnotherapy, Stage Hypnosis & Complete Mind Therapy" available from same source as this book or from Amazon, then you will be able to put people into Hypnotic States by getting them to stare at their own navels!

That perhaps could become your own personal marketing gimmick as you become "The Belly Button Hypnotist" and make a fortune helping people to cure their habits, Fears, Phobias and emotional problems by Staring at their own Belly Buttons as you place them into a Trance.

Now for some History and background information on the Human Belly Button which has been collected from various Public Domain Internet Sites including, but not limited to the following sites all of which you are recommended to personally visit for even more useful information and inspiration:

http://www.harpercollins.com.au/drstephenjuan/news_navel.htm

http://www.serenapowers.com/unusual.html

http://www.abc.net.au/science/k2/lint/facts.htm

BELLY BUTTON NAMES

The belly button has many names, including the fairly technical term "navel". "Navel" comes from the Anglo-Saxon word "nafela".

The Romans called the belly button the "umbilicus".

The Greeks called it the "omphalos". So if you add the Greek word "tomê" (meaning "cutting"), you get "omphalotomy". This word means "cutting of the umbilical cord".

Omphalos also means "knob" or "hub". The Greeks erected a holy stone, or fetish stone, in the Temple of Apollo at Delphi (on the slopes of Mount Parnassus near the Gulf of Corinth). They called this rounded conical stone the Omphalos (or Navel), as they thought that it marked the exact centre of their universe.

The tallest mountain in Bali is Gunung Agung. One Balinese myth says that their deities had mountains as their thrones, and that the highest mountain of all was Gunung Agung. The Balinese call this mountain the "Navel of the World".

The original inhabitants of Easter Island called it "Rapa Nui" ("Great Rapa") or "Te Pito te Henua" ("Navel of the World").

NAVEL-GAZING

The phrase "contemplating one's own navel" has the ring of a long and honourable history behind it. The word "omphaloskepsis" (also called "omphaloscopy"), meaning "contemplating one's navel as an aid to meditation", sounds like it is thousands of years old.

"Skepsis" is a Greek word meaning "the act of looking, or inquiry". However, the Merriam-Webster web site "Word of the Day" column claims that omphaloskepsis was invented only in the 1920s.

This was not the first time people tried to find enlightenment in the navel. In the past, an "omphalopsychic" was one of a group of mystics who gazed at their own navel so as to induce a hypnotic reverie.

The Greek Christian monks of Mount Athos used a specific method of navel contemplation called Hesychasm, to maximise the divine enlightenment. This method would presumably have given them many different insights into divine glory.

But another navel divination method, "omphalomancy", gave only one specific item of information. It predicted how many children a woman would give birth to, by counting the number of knots (bumps in the fleshy plaiting) in her umbilical cord when she was born.

BELLY BUTTON SCAR

Your belly button is your very first scar. It's scar tissue left over from where the umbilical cord joined you to your mother's placenta when you were in her womb. Just like fingerprints, no two belly buttons are alike.

All the nourishment going to the baby and all the wastes coming out passed through the belly button, via the umbilical cord. Once you had been delivered, your umbilical cord was usually clamped or tied, and then cut. The stump withered and fell off after a few days, leaving behind the scar we call the belly button.

Your abdominal wall is made up of various layers, including skin, muscle and fat. They are all fused together at your belly button. You have subcutaneous (literally, "under the skin") fat that plumps up the skin all over your body. But the fat cannot lift the skin at the belly button, because the skin at that location is fused to your abdominal wall. That's why the belly button is concave.

The umbilical cord is made up of four different structures : there are two arteries (taking waste to the placenta), one vein (supplying oxygenated blood and food), the allantois (which degenerates and turns into the bladder) and the vitello-intestinal duct (which turns into the gut).

PLACENTA & UMBILICAL CORD

Until the baby is born, it relies almost entirely upon the placenta. The placenta is a strange, flattish organ that acts as a combination of liver, kidney, lungs and intestines.

The placenta supplies the baby-to-be with oxygen and all the nutrients needed for growth. At the same time, it is a barrier that separates the baby from the mother.

It grows on the inside of the uterus and lies entirely outside the baby's body. (When I was a medical student, I decided that the uterus was my favourite organ, because of its wonderful design features.)

The placenta is where the baby's blood dumps all its wastes and picks up nutrients. It looks a little like a small, flat cake ("placenta" is the Latin for "cake"). It's about 20 cm across, 3 cm thick in the centre and much thinner at the edges.

The placenta keeps the blood vessels of the mother quite separate from the blood vessels of the baby. However, the blood vessels of the mother and baby run so close to each other that chemicals drift straight through the blood vessel walls.

Nutrients travel from the mother's blood vessels to the baby's, and waste products go in the other direction.

Even though the placenta is only the size of a small cake, it has a total surface area of about 13 square metres to ensure efficient exchange of nutrients and waste products. At birth, it usually weighs roughly one-sixth of the weight of the baby - about 500 grams.

But the placenta is also a very hard-working organ. At full term, it makes about 7.5 grams of protein each day. No other organ in the human body makes that much protein.

The umbilical cord is the lifeline that runs from the baby's belly to the placenta. It's a twisted structure about 2 cm in diameter. It increases in length during the pregnancy.

On average, at birth, the umbilical cord is roughly as long as the baby, 50-60 cm, but it can vary between 12 and 152 cm. If it is too long, there is a risk that a loop of the umbilical cord could get caught around the baby's neck as it enters the outside world, strangling the baby in the process.

One umbilical cord was so long that it "looped once around the baby's body, then over the shoulder, under an armpit and twice around the neck, with a good length left over to its root in the placenta". If the cord is too short, there can be difficulty in delivering the baby.

Before you were born, the umbilical cord, with its two arteries and single vein, was your lifeline. The power supply to push the blood to and from the placenta was your tiny foetal heart.
The two umbilical arteries carried low-pressure, de-oxygenated blood, loaded with waste products, through your belly button from your body to your mother's placenta.

The single umbilical vein carried high-pressure, oxygenated blood, full of nutrients, back in through the belly button.

(This is one of the rare cases where arteries carry de-oxygenated blood. Another one occurs in the lungs. Here the pulmonary arteries carry de-oxygenated blood from the right ventricle of the heart to the lungs - and pulmonary veins carry the red oxygenated blood back into the heart's left atrium.)

The blood moves through the umbilical cord at around 6.5 kph. At full term, about 1 litre of blood flows through the umbilical cord every minute.

About one-fifth of babies come out with the umbilical cord around their neck. Modern foetal monitoring techniques can warn the obstetrician or midwife of this occurrence.

After the baby is delivered, it still has the umbilical cord connected to the placenta. The placenta cannot be left inside the uterus - like the baby, it also has to be delivered. If the umbilical cord is too short, as the baby is delivered, it might pull the whole placenta off the uterus before it is "ready" to let go, or tear it apart. The baby could then die from massive blood loss, as its blood drains out through the umbilical cord.

UMBILICAL CORD SURVIVES INTERNALLY AFTER BIRTH

The umbilical cord forms in the foetus's second month of life. It contains four main structures, all running through the belly button. They are the pair of umbilical arteries, the single umbilical vein, the allantois, and the vitello-intestinal duct.

Early on, most of the allantois disappears. Inside the baby's body it turns into the bladder.

The vitello-intestinal duct is a structure that ultimately turns into the gut. By the time the growing embryo is just six weeks old, the vitello-intestinal duct has disappeared from the umbilical cord - 98% of the time.

After the baby is delivered, the four structures of the umbilical cord shrink and close up entirely. They turn into internal tendons or cords.

The two obliterated umbilical arteries run downwards to become the lateral umbilical ligaments, which join with the arteries supplying the bladder.

The obliterated umbilical vein becomes the ligamentum teres, which runs upwards and attaches the liver to the belly button. The obliterated allantois is now a cord that runs down to the tip of the bladder.

Once you've been an air-breathing baby for a while, there should be no connection between your gut and your belly button. But the vitello-intestinal duct can occasionally remain open along its whole length, or just part of its length, up until birth. Very rarely, it remains open past the birth and into adult life.

There are three main outcomes, depending on which section remains open. Sometimes it can discharge mucus or faeces. Sometimes it can form a little cyst behind the belly button. And sometimes it can even form a band that knots around part of the gut, and causes a life-threatening obstruction of the intestine.

About 2% of the population have a Meckel's Diverticulum. It's a little tube located on the front border of your ileum (part of your small intestine). The Meckel's Diverticulum reaches towards the belly button, but doesn't quite make contact.

Bailey and Love's Short Practice of Surgery says that the "*umbilicus is a creek into which many . . . streams may open . . . an enlarged inflamed gall bladder . . . may discharge gallstones through the umbilicus. Again, an unremitting flow of pus from . . . the umbilicus of a middle-aged woman led to the discovery of a length of gauze overlooked during hysterectomy five years previously*".

BELLY BUTTON SHAPES

In medicine and surgery, a "symptom" is something that the patient complains of, eg, "I urinate a lot and I'm always thirsty." A "sign" is something that the doctor would notice, such as yellowish tissue near the eye.

Hamilton Bailey wrote a famous textbook devoted to signs, Demonstrations of Physical Signs in Clinical Surgery. He included many of the signs of the human body that he could describe and/or photograph.

He became strangely poetic when he wrote that "*every time an abdomen is examined, the eyes of the clinician, almost instinctively, rest momentarily upon the umbilicus. How innumerable are the variations of this structure!*"

ROYLE NOTICE

Dr. Gerhard Reibmann, a Berlin psychologist, sees the belly button differently from Hamilton Bailey. He believes that you can diagnose a person's life expectancy, general health and psychological state purely by looking at their belly button. He paid for the publication of his own book, which he called ***Centred: Understanding Yourself Through Your Navel.***

All of my Internet Searches regarding this book have so far only found articles and comments about it from between 2001 & 2004, which is very interesting as I've been doing Belly Button Reading as a Navel Psychic for almost 15 Years (since 1990) and have been extensively featured in International Media doing so since 1996.

And perhaps most interesting is the fact that the information on Belly Button Reading inside this book was written by me and has been on sale as a CDROM since the year 2000.

Now I may be wrong but this seems to indicate that my creation and information on the subject has inspired other people, I say this because on various Internet Sites there is an extract from his book which seems to have been released (after my secrets went on sale) and the examples given are practically identical to those I give in the first chapter of this book – perhaps co-incidence – perhaps not?

And even if its not down to my book, much of this information was published from 1996 onwards in international media publications who did feature articles about me, so it would be logical that these article's could easily have been the source of Dr. Gerhard Reibmann practically identical to my approach information.

Either way it gives an apparently more believable & credible documented background from which to gain Media Exposure as a Belly Button Psychic.

Read this Extract From: *Centred: Understanding Yourself Through Your Navel* and then read Chapter One of this my book and tell me if you notice any similarities..

In it, he reckons that there are six different types of navel. He claims that each one has a specific personality type and a specific life expectancy associated with it.

It's easy to be sceptical of something this "easy", although it may turn out to be as inaccurate as phrenology (diagnosing character type by feeling the lumps and bumps on a person's skull).

Gerhard Reibmann, a Berlin psychologist, claims that if you have a horizontal navel (spreading sideways across your tummy), you're likely to be highly emotional, live for only 68 years.

But if you have a vertical navel that runs up and down your belly, you'll magically be generous, self-confident and emotionally stable. Somehow, this means that your life expectancy will be around 75 years.

A person with an outie, or protruding belly button, is claimed to be optimistic and enthusiastic and will live for 72 years.

However, a person who has a concave, bowl-shaped navel will be gentle, loving, cautious, delicate, sensitive and rather prone to worrying. Presumably, this worry will take a toll on their health, so they'll have the shortest life expectancy of all - only 65 years.

A person with a navel that's off-centre is supposed to be fun-loving and to have wide emotional swings. They're expected to live for only 70 years.

The final (and luckiest) type of navel is the evenly shaped and circular navel. This person is modest and even tempered and has a quiet, retiring personality - and as a result will live for 81 years.

Now, as we all know, anything to do with the human body always turns out to be more complicated than you first thought. How long will you live if your navel fits more than one of the six categories?

Easy, according to Gerhard Reibmann - just add the number of years together and divide by the total number of categories to work out your personal life expectancy.

The average life expectancy in Australia is 83.2 years for women and 77.2 for men. I guess that a lot of Australian women must have navels that are rounder than round.

LITERATURE & BELLY BUTTON LINT

The blue colour of Belly Button Lint is specifically mentioned in The Troublesome Offspring of Cardinal Guzman, by Louis de Bernières.

A town is being held under siege by bloodthirsty and cruel religious crusaders. Elders from the town go and ask a mad Englishman, Don Emmanuel, for his advice on how to annoy the crusaders as a form of guerrilla warfare. In his reply, Don Emmanuel speaks of BBL as "dingleberries". Strangely, he admits that he does not perform his own BBL removal, but has Felicidad do it for him . . .

"Don Emmanuel grinned, scratched his rufous beard and then

his pubic region, and said, 'I will give you all the advice in the world if only you can tell me why it is that the dingleberries excavated from my navel by Felicidad are always composed of blue Lint, when I possess no clothes of that colour.' "

Extract from The Troublesome Offspring of Cardinal Guzman by Louis de Bernières, published by Secker & Warburg. Used by permission of The Random House Group Limited.

CANCER & THE BELLY BUTTON

Very rarely, a secondary cancer can be found in the belly button. It's called a Sister Joseph's Nodule, or Sister Mary Joseph Nodule, in honour of Sister Joseph of the Mayo Clinic.

Sister Joseph had an observant clinical eye for patients and their lumps. She had honed it very finely indeed, over a period of very many years. In particular, on a few occasions, Sister Joseph had noticed that a certain type of lump in the belly button would later be associated with a cancer.

This cancer would usually be in its late stages. She told this to Dr William Mayo, who agreed with her. Her "sign" now has a permanent place in surgical history.

ADAM & THE BELLY BUTTON

In the Christian Bible and the Jewish Torah, Adam is the first man and Eve is the first woman.

The existence of Eve is explained in Genesis 2:7 and 21-22, which says: "*7 And the Lord God formed man of the dust of the ground . . . 21 And the Lord God caused a deep sleep to fall upon Adam, and he slept: and he took one of his ribs, and closed up the flesh instead thereof; 22 And the rib, which the Lord God had taken from man, made he a woman, and brought her unto the man.*"

Things get even more complicated with the creation of Adam. His belly button gave rise to many philosophical problems.

Some theologians have argued that because he was the first man he had no human parents. Therefore he did not come from a mother, did not have an umbilical cord and did not have a belly button.

And surely, they claimed, God would not give us the false impression that Adam (and Eve) came from a mother. But other theologians disagree. So what was a painter of 500 years ago to do?

Some painters took the easy way out, and covered the belly button area with a strategically placed fig leaf, tree or forearm. But braver painters such as Raphael and Michelangelo gave Adam a navel.

In fact when Michelangelo painted Adam on the roof of the Sistine Chapel in the Vatican he gave him a navel - where any worshippers, including the Pope, could easily see it.
One of today's radio preachers has condemned Michelangelo as *"immoral and unworthy of painting outhouses and certainly not worthy of painting ceilings"*.

Half a millennium later, in 1944, Adam's navel was a problem to a subcommittee of the US House Military Committee (chaired by Congressman Durham of North Carolina).

His subcommittee refused authorisation of a 30-page booklet, *Races of Man*, that was to be handed out to American soldiers fighting in World War II. The original booklet had an illustration that showed Adam and Eve each with a navel.

The subcommittee ruled that showing Adam's and Eve's navels would be "*misleading to gullible American soldiers*". It makes you wonder how the soldiers dealt with the horrors of war.

BELLY TO BREAST

Plastic surgeons are now able to insert breast implants via the belly button. The advantage of this is that it leaves no obvious scar.

The surgeons cut in through the belly button, and insert an endoscope tube under the skin. They work their way over the ribcage until they get to each breast, and then make an opening between the breast and the ribcage. They then insert a rolled-up breast implant into each breast. Once it's in place they fill it with salt water.

INNIE vs OUTIES

Your normal belly button is concave, with an attractive upper hood. The base of the belly button usually joins onto the muscle wall of the abdomen. Around the belly button there is subcutaneous fat. In the "outie", there is a protuberant mass of subcutaneous scar tissue between the bottom of the belly button and the muscle wall of the abdomen. This scar turns the concave "innie" into a convex "outie".

DRIER LINT IS A CANARY

In the old days, coal miners would take a canary down the mine. Canaries were exquisitely sensitive to some of the dangerous gases. If the canary keeled over, they'd leave the mine.

The lint from your laundry dryer could be a modern-day canary, according to Peter G. Mahaffy from the King's University College in Edmonton, Alberta, and his colleagues.

Back in 1994, the Edmonton Board of Health became concerned about high lead levels in the child of a radiator mechanic. Many of today's car radiators are made of various synthetic plastics. But back then they were made of copper pipes, and fins were soldered onto the pipes using a lead solder. (As the air went over these fins, it took the heat away.) So a radiator mechanic's regular work involved contact with a lot of lead.

Dr Mahaffy realised that lead particles could make their way onto the radiator mechanic's overalls, and then via the family washing machine into the rest of the family's clothes - and into their bodies.

The group tested the clothes dryer lint from radiator-shop employees, and compared it with the lint of people who had no known exposure to lead. The radiator-shop workers had dryer lint with lead levels up to 80 times higher than non-radiator-shop workers.

This is a rather neat screening test for lead. In general, the lead test involves drawing blood, which many children don't enjoy. Screening for lead by examining dryer lint is far cheaper and less invasive.

UMBILICAL CORD & BARBERS POLE

The umbilical cord has bright red veins spiralling through its white Wharton's Jelly. We see it every day symbolised in the barber's pole.

HAIR TRACK DIRECTS JOEY'S

Marsupials give birth to their young outside their pouch. The joey (the baby kangaroo) has to find its way to the pouch, by following a "track" in the fur of the mother kangaroo. Inside the pouch lies the source of life, the nipple. Is nature giving us a clue about the origin of BBL? The joey follows the hairs; does BBL take the same path?

BELLY BUTTON CLEANERS

A few different people sent in Belly Button Dusters. I didn't know that these devices existed before our survey. They have one job only - to remove BBL from your belly button.

One person sent in a small article from the *South China Morning Post* (10 September 2000) which tells of a different style of belly button cleaner.

This Stick-on Belly Button Cleaner is a Japanese invention. It's an adhesive pad which you apply *"over and into the offending area, and then remove it after 10 minutes (making sure you dispose of the evidence discreetly)"*.

They're available from the Lung Shing Dispensary Company in Hong Kong at a cost of HK$48 for six adhesive strips. I reckon it'd be cheaper just to yank the lint out manually - or you could use a friend's or relative's electric toothbrush . . .

GREEN BELLY BUTTON LINT – (BBL)

Zev Ben-Avi was in the military for 27 years, and is currently an advocate for the Vietnam Veterans Motorcycle Club of Queensland. He wrote to me telling me that *"in all my time, I never saw 'blue' Belly Button Lint, only green - jungle green, as in issue-type singlets"*.

However, he is not convinced that the lint comes from the clothing alone. *"To ease the situation with the troops, I found that intellectual activities in the form of apparently inane questions often occupied hours of funny but pointless debate.*

Obtain three army issue, brand new, jungle green athletic singlets. Weigh them very carefully on a precise machine that will register small but accurate increments. Record these weights on paper and then log the wash, wear and store cycles as they are rotated daily.

Every morning and evening, collect and carefully store the Belly Button Lint that has accumulated.

After about 12 months, again weigh the accumulated Belly Button Lint (which is GREEN, not blue) and again weigh the three singlets. The singlets will not have depreciated in weight and the accumulated Belly Button Lint will approximate the weight of one singlet.

The question then remains as to where the 'green' Belly Button Lint comes from. The questions to be asked are:

1. *If the Belly Button Lint is not from the singlet, then where did it come from?*
2. *If the Belly Button Lint comes from the singlets, then why do the singlets not decrease in weight?*
3. *If the Belly Button Lint does not come from the singlets, then why is it green???"*

I agree with him that BBL still grips tightly onto a few mysteries.

ANIMALS & BELLY BUTTONS

All mammals have belly buttons. However, in some dogs and cats, they're a little hard to see because they've healed well and they are covered with hair.

BELLY BUTTON REFERRED PLEASURE & PAIN

Leanne rang in to my Science Talkback show. She wanted to know why up until a year earlier, whenever she touched her belly button she had felt a pleasurable sensation in her clitoris. Unfortunately, after she had a laparoscopy (which went in via her belly button) she stopped feeling pleasure in her clitoris. In fact, she wondered if she would ever get it back again - because it felt pretty dang good.

The email response was huge. Both Katie and Sharon had had experiences similar to Leanne's. Luckily, their laparoscopies left them with some (but reduced) pleasurable sensation.

KF said that she also got pleasurable clitoral sensations when she scratched the lower half of her belly button really deeply. However, KS said touching her belly button made her go to the toilet. J said that the sensation was more painful than pleasurable. L said that scratching her belly button gave her a sensation in her right forearm (but only after she had broken her right elbow).

Greg said that touching his belly button made him nauseous - but only after sex. Jason got a sharp pain in the end of his penis when he scratched his belly button. Rick experienced an unpleasant sensation in his penis while being tattooed around, and partly inside, his belly button.
In reading all the emails, it seemed that most women enjoyed the belly button stimulation, while most men did not.

This seems to be a case of referred sensation. Imagine that both the navel and the genitals send sensation signals to one certain part of the brain. If you stimulate the navel, that certain part of the brain gets the same sensations as if you had stimulated the genitals.

However, I have not yet been able to find any references to the nerves of sensation from the navel and genitals being linked in this way. We can only hope that we will become further enlightened in this area.

MORE NAVEL HISTORY

According to Chinese lore, the best belly button is a concave one, rather than a protruding one, and the deeper the belly button the more children you will have. In these days of reliable contraception, the prediction relates more to the ability to have many children, rather than the inevitability.

Dreaming of your own belly button is traditionally associated with starting up a new venture with possible long-term benefits, and dreaming of someone else's navel denotes a new love affair.

According to Indian Tantric lore, the belly button is also used to diagnose health problems. Following this system, the navel is where energy is received and processed coming in from the universe.

The belly button represents fertility and it is also a reminder of the connection between the generations, in other words it connects you to your past and future. It is also seen being the "centre" of human beings.

The second form of omphalomancy is based on the umbilical cord. A Jamaican old wife's tale holds that the number of knots in the umbilical cord of a newborn baby shows how many more brothers or sisters are yet to come. It is interesting that this one has been verified and it seems to be accurate.

Apparently "Omphalomancy" is the Scientific Sounding Mumbo Jumbo name for Belly Button Reading and Navel-Gazing.

SUMMING - UP

So as this chapter illustrates there is far more to the Human Belly Button than many people realise and its this "genuine" information.

Good Luck & Enjoy

**Dr. Jonathan Royle – BSc
www.hypnotherapycourse.net**

CHAPTER TWO

NAVEL-GAZING

(The Bizarre Paranormal Art of Psychic Belly Button Reading)

My Unique & Bizarre Paranormal talents of Psychic Belly Button Reading, Healing and Mind Reading have enabled me to meet some of the worlds leading celebrities whilst earning a fortune into the bargain.

Becoming a regular face on National & International TV & Radio shows, whilst regularly being featured in Newspapers and Magazines making predictions for some of the worlds leading household names has just been an added bonus, and after reading this manual you too will be able to achieve all these things!

Navel-Gazing is the name I have given to my bizarre talent of examining a person's Belly Button to reveal their Past, Present and Future.

Navel-Healing is the name I gave to my demonstrations of how "Psychic Healing" can be achieved through the use of a Quartz Crystal placed into the subjects Belly Button.

And Navel-Mind Reading is the name for my experiments in Mind Control and Thought Reading which are all achieved by studying the persons Belly Button which you tell them is one of the most powerful Psychic areas of their body!

NAVEL-GAZING

Navel-Gazing which is the technical name for Psychic Belly Button Reading is a way of examining a human beings Navel in order to reveal their Past, Present and Future!!

Navel-Gazing is based on beliefs and experiences, which are hundreds of years old, including those of The Native American Indians.

The Native American Indians have a Religion called Shamanism and amongst their many beliefs is the fact that we all have Seven main Psychic Energy Points in our body called "Chakras".

The Chakra most commonly used by Psychic Readers and most often talked about by the public is the Chakra located in the centre of our foreheads which is often referred to by many as "The Psychic Third Eye!"

However my studies showed me that there is a Chakra almost perfectly in line with the Human Navel, and this Chakra which is called "The Base Chakra" is the Chakra (Psychic Energy Point) used by me for Belly Button Reading.

Interestingly enough it is also the Base Chakra, which is almost in line with the Navel that is spoke about in The Karma Sutra and in many publications on Tantric Sex.

Apparently if both the male and female imagine the energy from their Base Chakras being transmitted from their Navels and joining together with the energy stream being sent out of their partners Navel, then the sexual experience will be out of this World as will any Orgasms achieved.

As my studies revealed, most all forms of Psychic Divination have the reader tap into some form of Psychic Energy Source in order to gain their inspiration and information for the readings and indeed much the same thing is done in Navel Gazing.

I decided that whilst you could tap into the other Chakras and Energy points within the Human Body I would use the Base Chakra located almost perfectly in line with the Navel as this is the point to which you can get closest by physically sticking your finger into the Volunteers Navel.

When in a relaxed state I discovered that the moment I placed my finger into a persons navel that it was rather like sticking a plug into its socket and energy would flow from the Chakra through the Navel and then up through my finger and into my body.

At this point images would appear rapidly on the Blank TV Screen which I had been imagining in my minds eye and it is these images and the meaning of them that I would then relate to the Volunteer with often stunning accuracy.

These Images would enable me to tell the Volunteer about Past, Present and Future Events in their life and then as a further convincer that this was a serious method of divination I would reveal their TRUE Personality to them and the audience.

In other words the person they really are inside and not the person they pretend to be and this makes for dramatic viewing.

I would reveal their True Personality thanks to the Unique and Individual Physical appearance and traits of each human beings Belly Button.

These Traits I have discovered through many years trial and error can be read rather like the lines and markings on the hand are read during Palmistry.

Indeed in much the same manner as the Human hand the Navel has dents, lines, bumps and other characteristics all of its own.

For example I have found that in general:

01) The more a Persons Navel sticks outwards, the more extroverted and confident they tend to be.

02) The more a Persons Navel sticks inwardly, the more introverted and shy they tend to be.

03) People with Navels that neither seem to stick outwards or inwards and instead seem to be level with their chest tend to have Split Personalities and are very unpredictable and often emotionally unbalanced indeed.

04) People with a Horizontal line/dent across their Navel tend to be very down to earth, they call a spade a spade and are very realistic and relaxed about life.

05) People with a Vertical line/dent across their Navel tend to be very headstrong (as line points to their head). They can be very stubborn indeed, they have one hell of a temper and when they lose it boy do people know about it. Once their minds are made up they won't listen to reason even if it means shooting themselves in the foot in the long-term.

06) People with lots of dots/dents in their Navel tend to be very stressed/worried individuals who then worry about the fact

they are worrying. Also this could mean they are very analytical thinkers and spend far too much time analysing things before coming to a decision.

Many people have said to me in the past that these theories are all well and good and my results often amazing but then they say "Doesn't the Navel just end up the way it is because of the manner in which the Umbilical Cord was cut off at birth?"

Well say I to these doubting Thomas's, this may be correct but my belief is that everything that happens to us from the moment of our conception through to our birth and right back to the death of this physical body are all predestined and set out as a matter of Fate/Destiny.

Therefore Fate/Destiny orchestrated the action of your Umbilical Cord being removed in a certain manner in order that your Navel would fit you like a Fingerprint and like a good picture would speak a thousand words about you – and its these "words" which are observed in Psychic Belly Button Reading.

The creator's of Navel-Gazing were two British Psychic's called David Williams & Alex Alexander (both being past spiritual names of mine – yes both people are me Jonathan Royle!) and Navel Gazing although developed in the late Eighties, first made its appearance in the UK National Media during 1996.

Since then Navel-Gazing has been featured in British National Newspapers such as: The Sun, The Star, The Mirror, The Sport, Sunday People and The Stage & Television Today amongst numerous others.

Of Navel Gazing past UK Media comments have included:

THE SUNDAY PEOPLE said in August 1996 that "It Proved to be Uncannily Accurate".

THE DAILY STAR said in January 1997 that "Navel Gazing has been used to make many successful predictions for top Celebrities!"

Navel-Gazing has also been featured in many glossy magazines such as Chat, Looks, Eva, Uri Gellers Encounters and The National Enquirer amongst others.

And that's not to mention the countless times Navel Gazing has been featured to date on British, Irish & German National TV shows, along with Major Radio shows World-wide including Comedy World Radio of USA, Radio on the Cello of Spain, BBC Radio Ulster (Ireland) and most all National Radio stations within the British Isles.

On British TV shows such as C4's "Big Breakfast", BBC One's "False or True", ITV's "Taxi", UK Livings "Live at Three", Granada Breezes "Psychic Livetime", Sky's "Zest Health & Beauty Show", Anglia TV's "The Warehouse", Ulster TV's "The Kelly Show", "Big Brothers Bit On The Side" and BBC's "Body Parts" show amongst over 90 (yes over 90) other Feature TV slots about Navel Gazing on British & European Stations between August 1996 and January 2013.

Notable achievements of Navel-Gazing include when its creator David Williams was featured in The Daily Star during January 1997 and it is documented in print that by examining The Spice Girls Belly Buttons he predicted that Geri Halliwell (Ginger Spice) would be the first to leave the group to follow her own solo career and further predicted that her solo career would not be totally successful until she became Britain's answer to Madonna.

Well she did become the first to leave the group and she didn't get a UK Number one until she appeared very scantily clad in one of her videos rather like Madonna did in her earlier career!

Secondly this Daily Star article of January 1997 Predicted that Victoria Adams (Posh Spice) would become married to a footballer and have a baby boy. Well once again these two things have become fact with her marrying David Beckham the Manchester United Footballer and having a baby boy which she has named Brooklyn.

Also an Essex Evening Standard article of late 1996 detailed how Psychic Navel Gazer David Williams had cancelled a press conference in Essex with Girl Band "Intrigue" because having looked at photos of their Navels he had predicted the IRA's Bomb Threats to London which brought the City to a standstill on the day in question.

Celebrities who have in person (face to face with me on TV) received the Navel Reading Treatment include: The Spice Girls, Frank Bruno (British Boxer), Miss Ireland 1996, Cleo Rocus, Cynthia & Brittany (The Sweet Valley High USA Twins!), Sharon Davis (Olympic Swimmer), Rory Bremner (Top TV Impressionist), Craig Charles of Red Dwarf fame, Julia Carling, Lowry Turner, Sean Meo, Bella Emburg (Blunder-Woman), Zoe Ball, Keith Chegwin, Lily Savage and numerous others.

Whilst Celebrities for whom I have been commissioned to read the Navels of for features in major media publications include: Madonna, Tom Jones, Cher, Claudia Schiffer, Sean Connery, Jeremy Beadle, Prince Charles and numerous others.

For Television, Radio and Live Stage Performances the Navel is examined in person assuming the celebrity is there in person, and indeed for some Media articles you may get to meet the Celebrity in person for the purpose of doing the reading and more importantly from the publications point of view, to get photos of you peering into that persons Navel as it both makes a great story for them whilst also being great publicity for you!

For TV/Radio shows where the celebrities cannot be present and for many media articles it will be easier if you are given good clear close-up photographs of the persons Navel to do the reading from.

Now obviously these taken from Photos readings will not be quite as accurate as if the person were with you in person, but they are possible both by looking at the visual characteristics of the Navel through a magnifying glass and also because of another belief which is strongly held by Native American Indians and followers of the religion Shamanism.

This other belief states that each time your picture is painted or your photograph taken that part of your soul, life-force or Spiritual Energy (call it what you will) is taken from you also and enters the pictorial representation of yourself.

This means that a small tiny fraction of The Base Chakras Energy is within the photo and as such you can still tap into this for inspiration during the reading, which in this case is very akin to the Psychic art of Psychometry in which you hold peoples personal objects to reveal things about them – well how more personal can you get than a photograph of themselves?

NAVEL-GAZING GAGS!

Both on TV/Radio shows and Live on stage you will find these Belly Button and Navel-Gazing related jokes well worth using. OK so they may not be hilarious but then again you're a Psychic not a Comedian so a little humour is better than none isn't it?

I've recently been given honouree membership to The Army because of my special talents. They've made me a member of The Navel Core.

I learnt Navel-Gazing off my Great Grandfather who worked as a Belly Button Reader for the Army during World War One!

He was the Head of NAVEL COMMAND!

Yes this strange talent runs in the family, my Uncle wanted to do the same as my Great Grandfather had done for the Army during the War – but they wouldn't let him because he has two Belly Buttons instead of one!! They said he'd have to join THE NAVEL RESERVE instead!!

Belly Buttons were originally called "done-it's". In fact they were called "done-its" for thousands of years ever since Jesus started to Christen people in the Bible! Oh yes its true, he'd dip them under the water, say his Holy blessing and then he'd tap them in the stomach like this (make visual movement of pointing your finger into someone's stomach around the area of the navel) and then he'd say "done-it!"

It's quite easy to learn Navel-Gazing, for example two obvious things to look for when examining someone's Navel are Body Jewellery and fluff! The presence of Body Jewellery tends to indicate they are not soft people who'd start crying if

they got a paper cut, whereas Fluff inside their Belly Button tends to indicate they don't have a bath very often!

I taught Navel-Gazing to a Circus Contortionist called Sarah last year, a few months later she died – her family told me they weren't surprised about it though as SHE HAD SEEN HER OWN END!

CHAPTER THREE

NAVEL-GAZING COLD READING

Well dear reader, its time for a confession and that confession is that whilst the physical traits of Navels have indeed proved uncannily accurate as detailed earlier, and whilst you will find the majority of the time that by sticking your finger into a persons Navel and then allowing images to jump into your head (using your intuition) and then saying the first thing that comes into your head, that this will often prove very accurate indeed, the truth is that as "Navel Gazing" is a fun past-time also, that on occasion I will also use elements of a technique called Cold-Reading!

However a few things are very much in your favour with Navel-Gazing which are not with other forms of Psychic Readings and these are as follows:

01) Navel-Gazing is used by me only Live on TV/Radio shows and on Stage or for use in Newspaper, Magazine or Internet articles about my talents. Therefore never do you need to talk more than five minutes maximum to any one individual and usually less than that is sufficient.

02) In otherwords you use Navel-Gazing to easily obtain FREE PUBLICITY for your more conventional Psychic talents and needless to say the clients these articles attract are then given only a brief Navel-Reading before going onto a more normal Tarot or Palmistry session with which you can go into far more detail and be more accurate with.

03) In the case of all Navel-Readings done I always casually find out what that persons Star Sign is and then its quite easy

with a basic knowledge of Astrology to waffle on convincingly and with often quite accurate results for a few minutes which will be attributed to you having studied their Navel.

04) On most all occasions you are asked onto TV/Radio shows you will end up reading the Navels of Famous Celebrities and these are the easiest readings you'll ever have to do. Firstly you will either already have a lot of knowledge about that Celebrity or a few quick phonecalls to friends before going on air will reveal a lot of background information of much use. Most Celebrities have very similar lifes and so once again a little observation of the news and gossip columns will stand you in good stead. And also best of all is the fact that I've found that on TV/Radio shows Celebrities very rarely disagree with anything you say thus making you sound correct as they know the name of the game is entertainment and they too have learned to play this game properly.

05) When reading a complete strangers Navel for TV/Radio shows you will often be sent to the "Green Room" (Hospitality) area together before going on air. In fact you can demand that this happens by saying that it takes a good five minutes of silent meditation to tune into the subjects "Base Chakra" energy point, they will then ensure you have time to do this before going on air so as not to bore viewers. This of course is bullshit and the truth is you have now got at least five minutes to have a casual chat with the volunteers and find things out about them which of course are then fed back to them in different words than those used by them once on air. This combined with knowing their star sign should give more than enough patter to fill the airtime.

06) Make much of your patter about Predictions for the FUTURE, as these cannot be disproved at the time of the reading. Whereas you give very sketchy details of past events you can see via their navels – here for future predictions be very

detailed, very precise and very enthusiastic about what you are saying – also use a little common sense. By this I mean that although future events cannot be proved or disproved until a later time, with a little common-sense you can get well over 50% of your future predictions correct as most people experience similar things in their life at one time or another.

07) Once again Celebrities are by far the easiest to do readings for whether they are with you in person for TV/Radio shows or indeed even if it is from photos for use in a Newspaper of Magazine article. Not only do most celebrities have very similar lifestyles but also some things can be predicted with almost 100% confidence for celebrities and to illustrate how common-sense is used I will give a few examples of how I have very successfully predicted things in the past – which needless to say once they have become reality I have then made all the Media aware of my predictions which were documented in print or over the airwaves some months earlier now having come true, whereas any errors are conveniently forgot!

I predicted in "The Daily Star" of January 1997 that Geri Halliwell (Ginger Spice) would be the first to leave the Spice Girls. I did this because Observation and Common-sense told me that she seemed to be the one who always did the most talking at press conferences and I felt that amongst a group of then Five young girls this would not be tolerated for long by them and indeed when sparks did start flying I felt Geri would not hang around long – AND I WAS 100% CORRECT.

I predicted in this same Daily Star article of January 1997 that when Geri left she would be the first to pursue her own solo career and that success would elude her until she became Britain's answer to Madonna. I said this because working on the premise she'd be first to leave The Spice Girls, I figured she would still want to go on performing hence the solo career

prediction. I Knew the press would give her a hard time and that Spice Girls fans would not be happy she had left – this combined with fact it was public knowledge Geri had once been a glamour model led me to make the success will elude her until she becomes Britain's answer to Madonna prediction! Here again I was 100% correct because it was not until the MI Chico Latino video in which she was scantily clad that she got a Solo UK Number One.

I predicted in that same Daily Star article of January 1997 that Victoria Adams (Posh Spice) would end up involved with a footballer and that she'd have a baby boy. Well I worked on the premise that Celeb's tend to date other Celeb's and that being a very young women at the time she would like other young women I know fancy a Sportsman or two! Logic went further and told me she'd have more chance being a Celeb of meeting the person she fancied and hence the prediction was made. Babies wise I figured she like other young women would get pregnant quite early on and as for saying a boy that was a 50-50% chance. However luck was on my side AND ALL THESE THINGS BECAME 100% TRUE!

I once predicted that Comedian Lee Evans would become a famous Comedy Actor which indeed he has in films such as "Mouse – Hunt" and "There's Something About Mary!" I made this prediction because quite simply throughout the history of TV and Cinema some of the best Comedians have turned their hand to acting with great success and as this seems to be a tradition in showbiz I figured the law of averages was on my side which indeed they were and it became 100% CORRECT!

To clear up the IRA Bombing of London prediction allow me to say this was a sheer fluke – but like any coincidence which can be used to your advantage you should milk it whilst you can like I did to get maximum TV/Radio and Media Coverage – as

the more you become a household name, the more your services will become in demand and ultimately the more you will be able to get for your services. The truth is the girl group "Intrigue" had rung me the afternoon before the press conference and said they wouldn't be able to make it because of other commitments. I sat down and decided that rather than losing face with The Essex Evening Standard I'd wait until their offices had shut that evening and then leave a strange message on their answerphone explaining that I would not be there tomorrow as planned. This I did saying something along the lines of my absence would be because I predicted that travel through London would be almost impossible tomorrow. Then coincidence of coincidences I turned the news on the next morning and London had come to a stand still due to IRA Bombing threats and needless to say the moment the Essex Newspapers team got to work and heard the message from me which their answerphone had timed and dated as being left the previous evening they took my words as a prediction of this Bomb and so a huge article validating my predictions was run in the paper. This taught me to always be very ambiguous when leaving answer messages for the media – as if they have many possible meanings as indeed mine did they can be manipulated to help your cause in many situations!

Hopefully these few explanations of past successful predictions made by myself in the British Media will have helped make it clearer to you what I mean about how easy it is to make good accurate predictions for celebrity clients.

Don't forget also that before appearing on TV/Radio shows or Live Shows with guest Celebrities or indeed before meeting these people for other Media interviews you would have been told who your subjects were going to be.

It is then a simple job to get onto the internet and visit some of that Celebrities fan club sites which quite often contain lots of little known information about the person, their past, their present and their future plans!

On many occasions I've acquired information on Celebrities which I am to meet the following day from Internet gossip sites and fan sites and then have fed this information to them by way of my Belly Button reading predictions.

More often than not the detailed nature of what I have then been revealing has stunned the celebrities in question and on one memorable occasion I told a famous female American pop star what the name of her next album would be (I'd seen lots of rumours on fan/gossip sites) and she was so amazed that she admitted that although it was not public knowledge (she must not have seen the websites) that she would admit this was correct. So don't underestimate the power of the Internet for obtaining information on clients for use in your Psychic Readings!

b) Magazines & Newspapers will occasionally require you to do readings from good clear photographs of the celebrities Navels. And here's your chance to really look good in the media as I did with National Newspapers such as "The Sunday People." Find out what fee they are prepared to pay you for doing the readings and whatever the amount say your fee is usually much dearer! However as you like their newspaper or magazine you will do it for this price if they meet you half way. You then basically get them to send you the photos of the Celeb's for each of which you write a short few lines prediction and then these are returned to them on condition that when the article appears they print you predictions within an article that says "We the Sunday People sent Navel Psychic Jonathan Royle some decapitated photographs of Celebrities!" Then it should clearly state "Despite not knowing who the celebrities were as we'd cut their heads off the photo's he made these stunningly accurate revelations and predictions!" Yes this may sound cheeky but sooner than lose an excellent feature story you can often get reporters to bend over backwards to help you and needless to say a story which appears like this leads to even more TV/Radio work and lucrative clients.

09) For those who decide to become Navel Gazer's it would be wise to keep a scrapbook of any Celebrity photographs you see appear in Newspapers or Magazines where the persons Navel is actually visible. The logic here being you can then really do a test conditions reading instead of faking it as detailed in point 8 above. You see Newspapers and Magazines when asking me to do articles for them have I've noticed always asked me to read the Navels of Celebrities whom are currently "Hot News!" Also as Celebrities very rarely appear in photographs where their Navels are visible, if you keep copies of those which appear showing Navels and build up your scrapbook – success will be yours! You can then get the publications to Genuinely send you decapitated photo's – but as there will only be so many Photo's for them to choose from and they all tend to use the same Photo Libraries the odds are that by comparing the headless photos with those in your scrapbooks that a match will be found as you recognise the clothing matches! Then having discovered whom the Celebrity is an accurate reading is easy to do and both readers and publication alike will be amazed as you have done it under apparently impossible test conditions!

10) Remember to say very little – but appear to say a lot. This is easy to do by using lots of long and detailed words, phrases and descriptions to describe something, which is actually very simple, and either applies to everybody or to most people at some time in their lifes.

For example I use phrases like "You've lost a little bit of your sparkle recently haven't you love?" If she says Yes I would continue "Yes I know you have, you've been feeling down haven't you?" – well here she's bound to say Yes as your only saying the same thing in a different way again!

Then Continue "Yes you've been worrying a lot – then worrying about worrying it's become a viscous circle but its about to end and life will be like a bed of roses again in the very near future – you will keep positive won't you love?" – again she'll say Yes so you sound to be getting things 100% Correct!

But look at what I said again and you'll see one of my favourite Cold reading techniques in action which is to say something which is detailed but then end it with a positive closed question which can only really be answered YES by the subject as to answer YES is in their own interest!

Answering yes to this closed question has nothing to do with whether the predictions and information contained within the rest of that sentence were correct or not – however the audience watching or listening will perceive the subjects answers of YES as validation that your statements and predictions are correct!

Obviously if she answered No to the very first question you'd shoot off in the opposite direction and say something like "Well I know you don't feel like you've lost any of your sparkle but others have noticed your working too hard – you will take a little more time for yourself from now on won't you love?"

Here once again the closed question technique is used and once again it's in her interest to answer Yes – don't underestimate this cold reading technique its very useful indeed.

11) Furthermore, the more often you can get your subjects to say YES to you – the far less likely they are to either say you are

wrong or indeed to even let the thought that you may be or are wrong enter their head – it is in effect mild brainwashing.

I always start readings by making it quite clear that "Whenever I ask you a question I want you to answer Loud and clear!" (Pause) "Just say YES nice and loud! – OK?"

This is perceived by them and the audience as telling them to answer clearly to questions – but at a subconscious level in their mind prompts them to answer YES to everything.

This may sound like fairytale stuff – but I've been using techniques like this for the past 15+ Years since I started doing Stage Clairvoyance shows like Doris Stokes and other famous mediums in 1990 aged 15 years old and these methods have always worked for me!

12) Next we'll discuss the use of Closed questions just a little bit more before explaining how I use the power of Open Ended Statements and Questions for Cold Reading Success.

Closed Questions are those which can easily be answered by just saying Yes or No, and as in the aforementioned examples these can be phrased so that it is in the interest of the subject to answer Yes.

To repeat what I've already said only moments ago, for which I make no apologies as this is one of the strongest ploys you can have as a Professional cold reader – closed questions can be used to make your readings seem super accurate.

This technique is especially useful to Psychics doing Live demonstrations on TV & Radio shows and also to Stage Clairvoyants who perform before a large audience.

To re-iterate what I've said already, deliver a long list of detailed sounding (yet quite general) predictions and apparently factual pieces of information to the subject and then end your rather long winded sentence with a closed question to which it is in their interest to answer Yes.

Then as everyone hears them reply YES, they perceive this as being the subject validating all the things you have said as correct when in truth they are merely answering the question which you ended your statement with.

Another example of a closed question being used in this way is as follows

"With my finger in your navel I'm being shown a picture of a Valley made up of lots of hills and this is symbolic of your life to date!"

"The hills are in various sizes and I believe this is showing me the ups and downs you've had throughout your life – You're a survivor aren't you?" (Its in their interests to say Yes as its good for their ego/pride to do so)

"Now I'm being shown a picture of a brick wall and I feel this is symbolic of the wall you put around you in new encounters with people – You've been hurt in the past when you've least expected it haven't you?" (This will be answered Yes as we all have been at one time or another – yet it sounds to all listening like this is a truly detailed revelation you're making!)

"Now I'm being shown you caught between the devil and the deep blue sea so to speak – I'm being shown an image of you stuck between two people"

"Now both these people are friends, they may be in a relationship together, but what is clear to me is that you have become piggy in the middle to them because you don't want to upset anyone. Would I be right in saying you don't like upsetting people especially your friends?" (who is going to say anything else other than Yes you are right?)

"Yes I can see it clearly, there are two people around you, it may be family but I'm more inclined to say its on a friendship level. And both of these two people have been asking for your advice – yes that's it you don't want to take sides with either of them as you value the friendship of them both. You do value your close friendships don't you?" (Again Yes will be the answer)

"I can see good things for you in the future, I'm being shown prosperous times ahead for you. In fact I'd go so far too say that your going to come into some money soon. Those things you have been dreaming of aren't so far away now you'll be getting them sooner than you think – You've had your mind set on something very special to you for several years haven't you? (we all have dreams/ambitions so the answer will be Yes)

I could go on for pages and pages, in fact for days and days with examples of how closed questions can be used at the end of statements of apparent fact and can be phrased so as to guarantee a positive Yes response but I would hope that the examples I have given will set you on the right track and get you devising ones of your own.

13) Next lets turn our attention to the use of Open ended statements and questions and how these can be used by the Psychic to obtain far more information from the client about their life and problems than even they realise they are giving you!

Then later on in the reading this information which they have freely given you without even realising how much they have said can be fed back to them in a different context and/or phrased differently and will be accepted by them as amazing insights from you into their life/problems!

Quite simply an Open ended Statement is a statement, which could mean almost anything and cannot really ever be pinned down as meaning just one thing – hence its meaning is OPEN!

And Open ended questions are quite simply questions which are phrased in such a manner that they cannot be answered by just a Yes or No response and will instead provoke the subject to give you a detailed answer and therefore far more information than you actually really asked for or they realise giving you.

An example of an open ended statement would be: "I feel that at times you get very stressed and yet in other situations you are a very calm, relaxed and peaceful person."

This is neither right nor wrong for anybody! It will always be seen as being right as both possible scenarios and options are contained within the same statement of apparent fact!

Therefore the fact the statement cannot be seen as either right or wrong makes it OPEN and so it will fit everyone in some way at some time and so people will always respond as though it is CORRECT!

In other words Open statements are ones where you tell the subject they are one thing and then tell them they are at times the direct opposite as well!

Or you tell them they feel an emotion in certain situations and then tell them the direct opposite of this situation/emotion within the same statement.

I hope you get the hang of it as Open statements are a very easy way of devising Cold Reading patter which will fit every person on this planet or as it is known in the Cold reading trade "Boiler-Plate".

Open ended questions are those which cannot be answered with just a Yes or a No such as these few examples which follow:

"Why do I keep being shown images of a property matter in my minds eye?"

(They cannot possibly answer with just a simple Yes or No to a question such as this and instead will have to give a more detailed answer. If they are involved with some kind of property matter then they will tell you exactly what it is and later on in the reading you can feed this information back to them in a different context – perhaps with reassuring words that all things regarding this matter will prove successful! However if they state that they have no knowledge of a property matter you would very easily steer off on another course as follows)

"To be honest it doesn't surprise me that as yet you are not aware of this property matter (this implies there will be one soon) however I can see this image so clearly that I can very confidently predict that within the next six months period property matters will become an important focus in your life.

I'm being told to warn you to consider all the options when this occurs and not rush in like a bull in a China shop! You will be careful when this happens won't you?"

Well that's one example of how to phrase an open ended question which as with all open ended questions will make one of two things happen, either:

A) They will have something going on in their life which relates to the subject matter to which you are asking the question (asking for more information) and this they will then freely explain to you in great detail as they feel you are already aware of it – or why else would you have asked the question? Then later in this same reading this information is fed back to them in different words.

B) Or they will have no knowledge of such matters raised – but will instead usually make you aware of other matters in their life of concern to them as part of their answer and this itself gives you information which you can return to later in the reading. You then turn this into a prediction for the future and as such either way it will only ever seem like an accurate statement/prediction on your part!

14) Also don't forget the physical traits of the Human Navel which are detailed earlier in this manual, as I genuinely have found for some uncanny reason that these things do seem to have applied to 99.9% of all the people I've done Navel Readings for to date. And on the very rare occasion that you get something wrong it is easily covered up by saying that in this persons case that physical element must be there to serve as a reminder of areas of their ego/personality/attitude that they would benefit from working on in the future.

15) The way that people react to being asked to show their Belly Button to everyone and also the way in which they react when you stick your finger into their navel speaks volumes about their personality. After all don't forget how close to intimate sexual areas of the body our Navels are, and the fact that for many people they are Erogenous Zones (sexual turn on points)! Is it any surprise then that some people are very shy about showing their Navels in much the same way, as they may be sexually very straight-laced? And in much the same way those eager to show their navels are often outrageous flirts with broad-minded interests and opinions on all things sexual. Common Sense will work wonders here, just bear in mind what I've said and you'll see exactly what I mean when you put it into practice.

16) Another ploy to make the reading more accurate is to half way through your predictions and comments ask the subject if they have any specific questions they would like you to try and answer? Just say to them "Well I'm seeing so much in your Navel and we have so little time together today so to speed things up for you, are there any specific questions or areas of your life you'd like me to look into?" This makes it sound innocent enough, you don't seem like your probing for help and needless to say their answers give you all the information you need to carry on the reading in a very specific and accurate manner.

17) Two last points on Navel Cold Reading and these are that a) whether you are a believer in genuine intuition and Psychic powers or not – please do trust your intuition. The method of seeing a blank TV screen in your mind and allowing images to pop onto it as mentioned earlier in this manual is not only a good piece of explanatory patter – BUT IT ALSO WORKS! OK so you might think I'm bonkers, but if I had a pound for every time I've been on TV and suddenly said the first thing that came into my head of a very detailed and specific nature with 100% CORRECT & SUCCESSFUL RESULTS – then I'd be rich!!!

b) Secondly don't forget that other options are also open to you in order to make a really good impression on very important TV shows such as the use of a Mentalists Impression Clipboard before the show goes on air! You could get the people who are to have their Navels read to write down on a slip of paper three things: 1) The most important memory they have from their past. 2) The most important thing going on in their life at present. 3) Their biggest dream/ambition for the future.

They are told this is being done, as it will help make things clearer in THEIR MINDS and EASIER FOR THEM when you get on air! In other-words it is portrayed that you've had them do this FOR THEIR BENEFIT!

You then tell them to fold up the slips which you make clear you have not seen (you can see what the clipboard says later!) and to hide them in one of their pockets as you WILL NOT be using these on air – no they have just been written out by the subjects to get things CLEAR IN THEIR MINDS.

The subjects will not think anything strange of this especially as you will make the main part of their readings up from Cold Reading methods, but along the way for each subject you can reveal thanks to the clipboard one very definite and very detailed item about their Past, Present & Future.

You end up looking amazing, the viewers or live show audience are never any the wiser about the use of the clipboard before the show, and best of all Belly Button Reading and your talents in the use of it look super accurate and so even more FREE TV/Radio, Newspaper & Magazine publicity can easily be obtained.

With reference to the use of a Mentalists clipboard to obtain information for your reading please refer to the psychology behind how I use one for Pawology in a later chapter of this manual!

The Questionnaire which you get them to fill in on the Mentalists clipboard could also contain the disclaimer for "Navel-Healing" which will be mentioned shortly whilst also asking for their contact details for use in further media features.

CHAPTER FOUR

NAVEL-HEALING

Next we shall turn our attention to Navel Healing or as it is also called Belly Button Psychic Healing.

Again this is based on The Native American Indians beliefs and religion of Shamanism, along with the seven energy points in our body called Chakras.

Once again the Base Chakra which is in line with the Human Navel is used, except this time it is used for the purposes of powerful Spiritual Healing.

To help heal someone's complaints once they have first been to see a conventional Doctor (as we neither diagnose nor prescribe) we use a small pointed Quartz Crystal, which is placed into their Belly Button in order to promote natural healing!

One end of the Quartz Crystal is placed into their Navel and the other end held by the fingertips of your left hand and then your positive psychic healing energy is directed through your body, into the crystal and then into the Base Chakra energy point in order to promote rapid healing.

The reason this works so successfully is akin to the beliefs of many other complementary medicines such as Acupuncture, within which the Chinese practitioners believe that all illnesses, diseases and mind/body defects are caused by energy imbalances within the person's body.

Therefore logic states that if we feed positive healing energy into the patients most powerful psychic energy point (The Base Chakra) that this will help correct those imbalances and as such lead to successful recovery in rapid time!

The use of the pointed Quartz crystal as a way to get some of your positive healing energy into the patient is for two reasons.

Firstly the Quartz Crystal itself is used extensively in other forms of New Age Medicine such as Crystal Healing and indeed it is openly known by the majority of the public how powerful Quartz Crystal's actually are and the power they do in reality contain. This is a genuine tangible power which they contain and is the reason why small pieces of Quartz Crystal are placed into the mechanics of most all watches, as it is proven that the 100% NATURAL ENERGY within them helps the watch run better.

Also in much the same way THE NATURAL ENERGY of the Quartz Crystal helps the Human Body to run better, hence many people wear jewellery containing Quartz Crystal as a preventative health measure.

Here in Navel-Reading the Quartz crystal is used to help accelerate THE NATURAL HEALING process!

The reason why one end is stuck into the patients Navel whilst you hold the other end with the fingertips of your left hand is twofold.

Firstly The Crystal helps to amplify the power and intensity of the healing energy which is sent from our body into the patients and Secondly by holding the Crystal with the left hand things are amplified even more as it is the left side of the brain which deals with all things Spiritual and Psychic.

Once the Crystal is in position in the patients Navel you have them close their eyes and imagine a feeling of warmth starting to enter their body which is symbolised by the colour orange in their minds eye.

You explain that just so long as they concentrate on this feeling of warmth and keep seeing the colour Orange brightly in their minds eye that healing will prove successful for them.

(This also puts the blame onto them if successful results do not occur as planned – you just blame it on their lack of concentration)

The Logic of getting them to focus on a warm feeling is quite simply that people do naturally feel better within themselves when they are warm.

And the reason you get them to see the colour Orange brightly in their minds eye is both because seeing it brightly is as proven in NLP a positive thing and positive thoughts lead to positive results, but also is because the colour Orange is a powerful combination of the colours Red & Yellow mixed together and as such is the most powerful colour of the spectrum.

Then you the Healer concentrate on a blue beam of light energy flowing from all the seven energy points (Chakras) in your body, down through your left arm/hand and into the Crystal before finally entering the patients body via their Base Chakra energy point.

You concentrate on Blue energy/light as this is the curative healing energy – Just think of The Blue Cross emergency service for animals and you'll remember this easily.

Results will often be instantaneous, although they are always told this IS NOT an alternative to conventional medicine and rather is COMPLEMENTARY medicine, which just helps to dramatically speed up the healing process.

(This statement covers you both legally and morally and ensures that they seek conventional medical treatment and/or continue with any prescribed medication until a conventional Doctor says otherwise)

However results will often be dramatic and instant or within a very short space of time (which can still be used for follow up media coverage by keeping a mailing list of all participants in your show that receive Navel Healing).

The reason success so often occurs so rapidly is because of the proven fact that 90% of all reported illness is psychosomatic (all in their mind with no physical cause) and it is probable that 100% of unreported illness is also psychosomatic.

In these cases of Psycho-Somatic illness, as the illness is being caused by the patients mind – so the cure lies in their mind also, hence it is true to say that if they believe this will work for them THEN IT WILL.

Those that believe will naturally set their mind to a different way of thinking and so the end result can be one of an often apparently miraculous Cure.

Combine this with the PLACEBO EFFECT, which again all comes down to the patient BELIEVING that the treatment will work and you can now see why Psychic Belly Button Healing can be so successful.

This success combined with the perceptively bizarre method of treatment is what will attract all the TV/Radio, Newspaper and Magazine interest as it has done extensively for me in the past.

To understand both how Navel-Gazing & Navel-Healing can be and are so successful may I strongly urge you to buy or rent the excellent film "Leap of Faith" starring Steve Martin as this film is almost a course in itself of how Psychic Readings and Healing are achieved with successful results and as Steve Martins Character says in the film:

"To answer your question of if I'm genuine or fake I say this, what's it matter how I do things – Just so long as the job gets done!"

This is a sentiment I agree with entirely and just so long as you get a signed declaration from any patients you treat with Navel Healing which states:

01) They agree (if they haven't already) to get a conventional Medical Doctors diagnosis and prescription as soon as possible.

02) They agree to continue seeing their conventional Medical Doctor and/or continue taking any medication which they may have been prescribed.

03) They agree to allow you to touch their Belly Button for the purposes of Healing. (This covers you from any potential assault charges!)

You are then covered both legally and morally as you will never be placing a patient into any danger and instead have their best interests at heart always.

This signed disclaimer also asks for their contact details and acts as your mailing list for people to contact for inclusion in future media features on Navel-Healing.

Their recovery will most times prove to be considerably faster after Navel Healing than if they had just had conventional treatment alone and again this is because of their BELIEF that it will help them which in itself can REVERSE many problems which were Psycho-Somatic (Psychologically induced).

One of the Key phrases I use is "Those of you with health problems who volunteer tonight will only receive truly successful healing IF YOU WANT IT TO WORK (in other-words if you believe) and if you use your powers of Intelligence, imagination and Concentration effectively!"

This Psychologically ensures that only those who BELIEVE that rapid healing will result will volunteer and indeed as such these in my experience usually tend to be the ones for whom it will work.

This Phrase also covers you for failure as if instant healing does not occur, which often cannot be proved one way or the other until the patient revisits their doctor, then the way it is phrased puts the blame for failure onto the patient.

You see the audience will just see it as failure on the patient's part for not using their powers of intelligence, imagination and concentration effectively as they were told to do!

It is in effect A FORM OF HYPNOSIS, except with Navel healing the patient HYPNOTISES THEMSELVES due to their own belief system telling them that this form of treatment will work for them!

IF THEY BELIEVE IT WILL BE SO –
THEN SO IT WILL BE

Well that basically is all there is to Navel-Healing as the rest is just down to presentation on your part. Present Navel-Healing with NO DOUBTS in your mind that it will work and then this positive attitude will be sensed by your volunteers.

When your volunteers sense this confident attitude within you that Navel-Healing will be beneficial to them then they will start to be even more positive about it working and so the magic of Positive Thinking comes into play.

And need I remind you of the countless books published and medical studies done on Positive thinking which have proved beyond doubt that positive thinking can often lead to CURES in and of itself.

So with the combination of Positive Thinking, Self-Belief of the patient, The placebo Effect, Self-Hypnosis and Psychic Mumbo Jumbo all combined into one treatment method, Navel-Healing is very powerful indeed.

Usually Navel-Healing would be done with the person there in person next to you, however for TV/Radio phone ins and media articles (or mail order sales) this can be got around by using a good clear photograph of the persons Navel.

The theory as to why this will still work regards the photo is the same as with Navel-Reading, however here you also speak to them in person over the phone and step by step explain what you are doing at your end.

It is also explained to the patient what they must do at their end as you concentrate the healing energy through the crystal into the photo of their Navel and due to some of the energy of their Base Chakra being caught in the Photo, then into their body for the same healing results.

This is known as "distance healing" and just so long as the patient believes it will work, then it will prove to be just as successful as if the person was next to you in person.

I will now explain a few visual demonstrations which can be used on TV and Live stage shows to demonstrate instantly how successful the technique of Navel-Healing is, and may I point out that if these demonstrations are carried out BEFORE any actual personal one to one healing is done then results will be INCREASED!

The reason quite simply being that once the patients to be have seen these visual demonstrations of how Navel-Healing works, then their BELIEF & FAITH in it working for them will be total.

WEAK ARM – STRONG ARM TEST

This is a visual demonstration which I have used along with the other tests which will be explained with great success in the past on TV shows including "Psychic Livetime" (Granada Breeze), "Live at Three" (UK Living) and Children's "Nickelodeon" TV Station amongst many others.

I have also used it extensively as a live demonstration piece both on Stage & in Cabaret and also whilst giving lectures at many of the Psychic Fairs which in the past I have attended and exhibited at!

EFFECT

Volunteer one clenches their right fist and then with their fist in this closed position places their right arm outstretched straight in front of them.

They are told to close their eyes and imagine clearly a time in their life when they felt very weak unloved & unwanted.

They are told to now notice how weak, how drained and how NEGATIVE this makes them feel.

"Feeling weak, drained and negative from the tips of your toes to the tips of your fingers!"

You tell them to TRY to keep their arm straight out in front of them as they allow these NEGATIVE emotions and feelings to flood their entire body from tip to toe.

Then you count to three: - 1,2, and on 3 you cue a 2nd volunteer upon the stage to push down the first persons right arm which they find they are able to do with the greatest of ease.

It is explained to the audience that under normal circumstances the 1st volunteer would have been able to keep his arm much stiffer, much straighter and out in front of him for much longer despite volunteer number two pushing down on his arm.

It is explained that this demonstrates how Negative emotions in our minds can lead to Negative effects in our bodies and as a consequence often lead to unnecessary illnesses and disease.

The good news however, is that by using a form of treatment such as Navel Healing we can remove all negative emotions from our bodies and therefore end up with a far more healthy life.

To demonstrate this you have Volunteer number 1 close their eyes once again, you place the Quartz Crystal into their Belly Button and have them imagine the warmth represented by the colour Orange that is now flooding into their body.

They are told that just so long as they see the colour Orange clearly that in a few moments time something which was just a few moments ago so difficult will now become so ridiculously easy to achieve.

They are told to notice the inner strength they now feel which is making each and every muscle group in their body from the tips of their toes to the tips of their fingers STRONGER than they have ever been before.

(You of course during this time also appear to do your bit of directing energy into their Base Chakra energy point whilst thinking of the Blue Healing energy!)

Volunteer number one is then told to resume the same position as before with their right fist clenched and their right arm held outstretched straight in front of them.

Volunteer number two is then told "OK on the count of three just TRY to push his arm down and notice how difficult it is for you and how much STRONGER he has become, 1, 2, 3, That's it just TRY to push down his arm.

Volunteer number two is allowed to continue TRYING for a few seconds or so and then is told to relax. Then volunteer one is told to relax also and take their new-found strength with them.

When asked volunteer one WILL SAY how weak he felt the first time and indeed how much stronger he felt the second time around.

Volunteer two when asked will genuinely comment how much more difficult she found it to get his arm to budge the second time around.

EXPLANATION

Everything is done and carried out 100% exactly as I have just explained, with only a few points being of particular relevance as follows:

The first time around volunteer one has to hold their arm out in front of them from the very start of the demonstration and so it is little wonder that their arm is tired by the time volunteer two comes to push it down.

Also the first time around the psychological effect of thinking of negative things will genuinely make volunteer one feel weaker – its quite simply a simple form of SELF-HYPNOSIS which makes this work without fail with any willing & co-operative subject.

The suggestion of "TRY to keep your arm out straight in front of you!" suggests by that single word TRY that they will be unable to do so!

This is a technique known in Hypnosis as "The Law of Reversed Effort" which states that the harder they TRY to do something the less success they will have!

And finally with reference to the first time round where volunteer one is made to feel weak, because you cue volunteer two to push their arm down on the count of three without person one hearing you it will then come as a shock when it happens!

Because volunteer one does not know when his arm will be pushed down or indeed expect it to happen at all, it will be a complete surprise to him when this happens, he will be caught off-guard and will not have chance to tense up his by now already very tired arm.

The moment this first demonstration is done both volunteers are told to relax as normal. This gives volunteer one time to rest his arm ready for the second time!

This time volunteer one stands with his arms by his side and eyes closed as you tell him to think of the positive times in his life when he felt STRONG, confident and on top of the world.

He is told to notice that as he clearly sees these things in his minds eye so at the same time he starts to feel STRONGER in each and every muscle group from the tips of his toes to the tips of his fingers.

You then start to explain to the audience that its time to make volunteer one much stronger and healthier by the power of Navel Healing and go into the usual Psychic Mumbo Jumbo at this point!

The moment volunteer one has started to visualise the colour Orange clearly in their mind, then and only then you get them to resume their original position of having their right arm straight out in front of themselves with the fist clenched.

Volunteer one is told "Notice how much stronger you feel, notice how much stronger you are and how much stronger you have become!"

Volunteer two is then told "On the count of three I want you to TRY and push his arm down as you did before, except this time notice how much harder it becomes for you to achieve this."

Then you count 1,2, and on 3 – Just TRY to push down his hand, that's it Just TRY, TRY (continue like this for a few seconds and then say) And now everyone just relax once again.

This time volunteer one has been warned when the pushing will begin and has time to tense their arm, also this second time around it is upon volunteer two that the Law of Reversed effort is used by suggesting to her to TRY and push down his hand.

SUMMING-UP

Do exactly what I have just explained in exactly the way I have said to do it and this demonstration will work EVERY time. Yes the levels of success will vary, but in general 9 times out of ten the visual difference will be VERY DRAMATIC!

And in the other 10% of cases it will still be visual enough to show that Navel-Healing has indeed made the man stronger the second time around.

This works due to a combination of The Law of Reversed Effort (TRY), the verbal suggestions given to them and the things they think of (self-hypnosis), and the fact that second time around the man (volunteer one) has prior warning of when the woman (volunteer two) will TRY to push down his arm.

He has of course also had a minute or two to rest his arm between tests and this time only places his arm outstretched in front of him at the last second, thus not giving it time to get tired as in the first instance.

This may not sound very impressive when described like this on paper, but visually its very dramatic and makes for a good TV or Stage Show demonstration which both the audience and those whom participate in the experiment will find AMAZING!

BUCKET OF ICE TEST

This is a routine, which I originally saw demonstrated by a so-called Conventional Psychic Healer called Mathew Manning on Uri Geller's ITV Special "Beyond Belief".

EFFECT

It is explained to a volunteer seated on stage, that in a few moments time their right arm will be placed into the fish tank next to them which is full of Cold Water and Ice.

They are told to remove their hand from the Iced Water the very second that they feel it is too cold or painful to keep their hand in it any longer.

They are told to close their eyes and you then lift up their arm and place it into the tank of Iced Water without warning.

From the second their hand enters the Water until the very second they remove their hand is timed by a stopwatch which is held and operated by a 2nd Volunteer from the audience.

The time is noted and Volunteer one is told how long they managed to keep their arm under water before the Navel-Healing begins.

Volunteer One is told to close their eyes and relax as you place the Quartz Crystal into their Navel and start the Psychic Mumbo Jumbo.

You suggest to them that "In a few moments time when and only when I count to 3, then and only then I will place your right arm into the water tank beside you."

"This time you will notice that from the very second your hand enters the water you WILL FEEL calm, relaxed and confident in every way!"

"You will notice that something you once thought would be so difficult now becomes so ridiculously easy and you will feel NO DISCOMFORT whatsoever!"

Then you go into the think of the colour Orange Blurb and feel the warmth Patter mentioning to the volunteer that:

"Just so long as you keep seeing the Colour Orange brightly in your minds eye whilst feeling that warmth flooding your entire body YOU WILL FEEL NO DISCOMFORT whatsoever and will be able to keep your hand in the tank for much longer with the greatest of EASE!"

1- Relaxed, Calm & confident. 2- feeling warm & strong inside and on 3 Just notice how, unlike last time you feel no discomfort whatsoever. (As you count three you place their hand back into the water)

At this point Volunteer number two starts the stopwatch and prepares to stop it the very second that volunteer number one removes their hand from the water again.

The times are compared and it is noticed with much amazement from both those involved and the audience that She was able to keep her hand under water for CONSIDERABLY longer the 2nd time around!

She is given a towel to dry her arm and returned to the audience to thunderous applause.

EXPLANATION

Basically if you do exactly what I have explained in the way I have explained it, and say what I have said in the way that I said it then this WILL WORK with great success for you.

The volunteer hypnotises themselves through their belief that Navel-Healing will work, as don't forget you asked only for volunteers who were willing & co-operate whilst having very good powers of Intelligence, Imagination and Concentration.

Your suggestions to them as detailed in the "effect" section are worded such as to Hypnotise them further into the belief that this will work.

The fact they have had their hand under the cold water once means that the second time around it is not so much a shock to their system and this alone will allow them to keep their arm under for longer than before.

Also second time around the idea of pain is NEVER allowed to enter their head. You see first time around they are told "Remove your hand from the water the very second it becomes too PAINFUL to keep it there!"

This suggests to them it will be painful and with this in their mind it won't be many seconds before they remove their hand from the water.

However second time around the word pain is NEVER ever mentioned and instead they are told to notice HOW LITTLE DISCOMFORT they will feel and how much easier it will be this time.

Lastly the fact they know how many seconds they kept their hand under first time around will usually make them determined to beat this second time around and in a focused state of mind such as this – SUCCESS WILL BE ACHIEVED.

For this experiment I find it works better if the volunteer with the stopwatch is a male whilst a female is used to place her hand into the water tank!

The tank by the way is nothing more than a reasonable sized fish tank, which is filled with 50% cold water, and 50% Ice cubes!

Incidentally it's a proven scientific/medical fact that women have a higher pain threshold than men and that's another reason why I use a woman for this "Bucket of Ice" test.

PSYCHIC STRONGMAN TEST

As a demonstration of Navel-Healing this experiment has been used by me on countless Television shows, and indeed this test is so good that it has been used by top psychic performer Uri Geller on many of his world-wide TV shows to date, although obviously Uri didn't present it as Navel-Healing as we will do!

EFFECT

A large volunteer is seated on a stool/chair and four other volunteers are asked onto the stage to participate.

The man on the chair is told to sit upright with his hands on his lap, whilst the four other volunteers are told to interlock the fingers of both hands so that the fingers of the left hand are against the back of their right hand and vice versa.

With their hands interlocked in this position they are then instructed to place their two Forefingers so that they point outwards with their fingertips away from their interlocked hands.

With their hands like this two people are told to place their outstretched forefingers underneath the seated volunteers armpits (one under his left armpit and one under his right).

And the other two volunteers are told to place their outstretched forefingers under the seated mans kneecap area, again one under the left side and one under the right.

On the count of 3 they are all told to TRY and lift the seated man as high as they can noticing as they do how difficult this is to achieve. 1,2,3 – OK just TRY.

They attempt to do this either with no or very little success, which demonstrates how hard the following test, will be to achieve.

The four volunteers who are stood up all overlap their hands in the air so they go, right, right, right, right, left, left, left, left in order so all four people now have their right hands on top of each other in the pile and then their left hands above these!

At this point you place the Quartz Crystal into each person's Navel and get them to concentrate on the Orange Colour and the warm feeling for a few seconds.

As you do this it is suggested to them all that "In a few moments time we are going to lift this man again and this time something you once thought would be so difficult WILL become so ridiculously easy!"

"Just so long as you think of the colour Orange at all times you will find that he becomes as light as a feather and that you become as strong as an Ox!"

"On the count of three I want you to all remove your hands from the pile and put your hands back together as they were before so that your fingers are interlocked onto the backs of your hands with only your Forefingers pointing outwards away from you.

Then immediately resume your positions as before, so your fingertips are under the mans armpits and kneecaps as you had them before and then the very second I shout NOW – that very second YOU WILL LIFT HIM UP with the greatest of ease.

1 – Confident, Calm & relaxed, 2- Strong as an Ox and on 3 Resume your positions this very second. (Allow them all to do so and then say) NOW – Lift him up – higher and higher and higher!

This happens and yes the man is almost thrown through the roof the second time to everyone's amazement, before being returned to his chair.

EXPLANATION

Don't even ask me to explain why this works – but believe me it does! I can honestly say that I've been using this test both on TV and Live Stage shows for a number of years now and it has NEVER gone wrong.

Admittedly the patter I use is worded following the rules of NLP and as such actually does have a positive psychological effect on the volunteers.

However even if you carry out this test without using the patter I've suggested then, as you will find for yourself, this test will still work!

The most bizarre thing about this test is that at the end the seated person will swear that they actually felt themselves get lighter, whilst the four other volunteers will swear they felt themselves get much stronger.

Don't underestimate the visual & psychological impact this test has on an audience as I have always found it to be an excellent applause puller, which is long remembered by the crowd!

CHAPTER FIVE

NAVEL MIND READING

I've taught you Navel-Reading and Navel-Healing, so now its time to reveal my secrets of Navel Mind Reading or as it is also called Belly Button Mind Reading!

Essentially this is just a way of presenting standard Mentalism effects in a manner which gives the audience the impression that you are reading the subjects mind by way of looking at their Navel for information.

You can present the routines of your choice as demonstrations of Navel-Healing in one of two distinct ways as follows:

01) You can look at the volunteers Navel whilst explaining that the Physical characteristics of their Belly Button combined with the vibes you get from the Base Chakra energy point will reveal the thing they are thinking of to you.

02) Or you can tell the volunteer that as they think of their randomly chosen word (or whatever the routine entails) that they are to hold up their shirt revealing their Navel. They are then told to imagine a Neon Light Beam projecting from their Base Chakra energy point, out from their Navel and out into the distance before them like a bright neon sign which displays upon it the information which you are about to reveal by Psychic means! You then reveal the correct answers as if you are able to see this psychically projected neon sign!

I'm sure you can already think of numerous routines, which could be presented as demonstrations of Navel Mind Reading, but for the sake of completeness I'll explain two of my favourites.

THE PSYCHIC PROVERB TEST

EFFECT

Five volunteers are each given a pen, a blank visiting card and a small brown wage envelope before being instructed to write down a well-known proverb or saying onto the visiting card.

The five volunteers are then told to seal their visiting card into the brown wage envelope, which they have also been given, and then to place all of them into a pile on the table.

Once placed upon the table another independent volunteer mixes up the five envelopes so that neither you, the audience nor the on stage volunteers have any idea what order they are in.

You then explain that by studying their Navels, which will reveal their true personalities, you will attempt to give back the correct visiting card to the person who actually wrote it.

They are all told to keep quiet and not say or do anything which would indicate if your choice is right or wrong until you have given all five of them a card and tell them to indicate if you are correct or not.

For the first time you get to touch the envelopes and one by one you open them and by studying each person's Navel in turn give back one card to each person.

At the very last minute you change your mind about two of your choices and swap around two of the cards between two of the volunteers.

Now its make or break time and you say "I'm going to count to three and on the count of three if and only if I've given you the correct card – namely the one which you yourself wrote, then and only then I want you to wave the card in the air and shout out as loud as you can – Jonathan Royle is the world's greatest psychic Hallelujah!"

1, 2, 3 (At this point all five wave their cards high in the air and shout out that you're the worlds greatest psychic which always leads to spontaneous applause from the audience)

EXPLANATION

Despite its simplicity this routine has served me well on TV shows such as ITV's "Funky Bunker", UK Living's "Live at Three", ATV's "The Warehouse" and on Children's "Nickelodeon" station amongst numerous others.

I've also used this routine for many years on my live stage shows and on several occasions have even tailored it for product launches.

For example I was doing a Corporate Product Launch for a new string of Indian Restaurants at the Telford Moat House Hotel during 1996 and instead of proverbs I got each person to write their favourite Indian food dish onto the cards from the choice available on my clients menu!

The effect was still presented as Navel Mind Reading, but in this way also helped to promote my client's product range and variety of different dishes.

As for how its done I'm sure you are way ahead of me, the envelopes are all marked enabling you to easily tell which card in each envelope was written by which person.

On Live Stage shows things are seen by the audience exactly as described under the "effect" section and so its vital you do things in the right way!

Have the five volunteers positioned in a straight line and from left to right hand them each an envelope, pen and blank visiting card.

Needless to say that the first person (person on left) gets the envelope marked number one, 2nd person gets envelope marked number two and so on until person number five (on right) gets the last one marked number five.

The dirty work is over now, you can turn your back and they can now write down their proverbs before sealing their cards into the envelopes, which they are holding.

They tell you when this is done, but instead of turning round straight away you have them place their envelopes onto the table and get another independent volunteer to mix up the envelopes so nobody could possibly know what order they are in or which one belongs to who!

At this point you turn round and now its all down to your presentation, as quite simply each time you pick up an envelope the marking upon it reveals to whom it belongs.

For example the envelope marked as being envelope number three would be given to the person third from the left in the line up of volunteers.

As for how do I mark the envelopes? Well I snip a small V (small triangular shape) into the seal down end section of the envelopes flap.

The V cut nearest to the left hand side with the sealed down flap side of the envelope held towards you denotes person one, whilst the V cut nearest to the right denotes person number five.

The V Cut dead centre denotes person number three and I'm sure you can work the rest out for yourself.

The advantage of using the V cuts rather than pencil dots or other marks is that as you pick each envelope up you just need to run your thumb across the edge of the sealed flap and you will feel where the V cut is on that flap.

This means that just by feeling the sealed down flap you can discover which person the contents of that envelope belong to and as such the need for looking suspiciously at the envelope is eliminated.

It's a good idea to give two of the cards back to the wrong people as psychologically it looks more impressive to realise your mistake at the last second and change them to their correct owners before discovering the impressive outcome.

For TV shows the preparation is all done before going on air, which means that you can make things seem even more like they are under test conditions.

Before the show goes on air you get the person who will be presenting your section of the show and the five volunteers to join you in the green room.

Here you hand each of the five volunteers a card, a pen and a wage envelope before explaining what they should do.

You then tell the presenter that once the five people have written down their things s/he should then and ONLY then mix up the five envelopes before placing them into their pocket for safe keeping until its time for their use on air!

You then leave the room and allow all this to be done without you even being present at the time, then on air you can stress how all this was done, you never went near the envelopes, don't know who wrote what etc.

Just so long as you are clear and forceful with your instructions to the volunteers before leaving the room then THEY WILL DO EXACTLY as you've ordered!

When performing this routine I tend to combine some cold reading into it, this means that as I examine each persons Navel to ascertain to whom I should give each card I also give them a brief Belly Button Reading of their past – present and future using the methods explained earlier.

THE BASE CHAKRA PROJECTS THE ANSWER

The routine, which follows, is one, which I originally devised in 1990 for use in my stage Clairvoyance shows, and then I called it "The Psychic Third Eye Projects the Answers!"

The routine and secret of operation were exactly the same with the only difference being that I got the volunteers to demonstrate their Psychic powers by projecting the correct answer to me through the Chakra energy point in the centre of their forehead known as the Third Eye!

Incidentally it was routines like this one, which gained me much exposure in International publication "Psychic News" and which saw them dub me "The New Uri Geller and Doris Stokes rolled into one!"

EFFECT

The venue manager is beckoned onto the stage and brings with them a plastic carrier bag, which is found to contain five newly purchased decks of playing cards & the receipt for their purchase.

The venue manager leaves the stage and a large foam ball is thrown into the audience over your shoulder to randomly pick another volunteer.

The person who catches the ball is told to come up to the stage and becomes the independent adjudicator on behalf of the rest of the audience.

They confirm that the bag contains five brand new decks of playing cards and are then asked to FREELY select any one of the decks from the bag.

The bag is now discarded and the on stage volunteer is asked to open the deck of cards, this they do by first removing the cellophane from around the box and then removing the cellophane from around the cards which are inside the box.

They are asked to remove the jokers from the deck which they now do and then are told to cut the cards as many times as they want so that nobody could know what order the cards are in.

You then instruct the volunteer to hand the deck face down to someone in the front row of the audience and this person is asked to thoroughly shuffle the deck of cards again in order to ensure they are randomly mixed.

The cards are then returned to the original volunteer who now proceeds to give one card to each of ten people in the front row of the audience whilst your back is turned.

At this point the volunteer can return to their seat and you can turn around to start this amazing experiment.

You tell each person holding a card to remember Just the number or letter which is on their card and to for now forget about the suit.

They are then told to lift up their shirts/jumpers etc in order that their Belly Buttons are uncovered enough that they can project energy from their Base Chakra Energy point.

You tell them to think of the number or letter which appears on the card they ended up with and to imagine this being projected from their Base Chakra energy point in a beam of psychic light rather like a bright blue neon sign lighting up the theatre.

You comment that lights are starting to come on everywhere and that the audience tonight are very psychic indeed and then you proceed to tell each person what number or letter of card they are holding.

As an encore you ask five of the people to stand up and this time they should try to project the suit of the card they are holding also.

You then amaze everyone by revealing the suits of the cards these five people are holding also, before telling them to keep the cards as souvenirs of their first psychic experience.

PREPERATION

On the day of your show go to a large store in the general area of the performance venue and purchase Five decks of playing cards with a mixture of different coloured backs and if possible back designs as well.

Ensure that you ask them for a carrier bag, which bears the stores name, and make sure you keep the receipt, which will also bear their name.

Return home and very carefully undo the flaps or slice open (using a razorblade) the cellophane flaps at the bottom end of the deck.

You will then be able to carefully remove the cellophane cover keeping it intact for replacement later.

The sticker, which seals the deck closed, is sliced through with a razor blade enabling you to open the box and the cards are removed from within.

You carefully undo one end of the cellophane and remove the cards from it, again keeping the cellophane until later.

The Jokers are placed to one side and the deck is now set up into the famous 8 Kings deck set up, which for those few who don't know goes as follows:

8C-KH-3S-10D-2C-7H-9S-5D-QC-4H-AS-6D-JC

8H-KS-3D-10C-2H-7S-9D-5C-QH-4S-AD-6C-JH

8S-KD-3C-10H-2S-7D-9C-5H-QS-4D-AC-6H-JS

8D-KC-3H-10S-2D-7C-9H-5S-QD-4C-AH-6S-JD

The order of the cards letters or numbers as referred to in the routine is easily remembered by use of the simple Mnemonic of:

Eight – Kings – Three – Tenned – Two – Save (7) – Ninety (9) - Five (5) – Ladies (Q) – For (4) – One (A) – Sick (6) – Knave (J)

And the order of the suits is easily remembered by the Mnemonic CHaSeD. Each of the capital letters in this word referring to one of the suits e.g. the order is Clubs, Hearts, Spades and then Diamonds.

At this point place the two Jokers and the extra Joker randomly into the deck and them carefully replace the deck into its cover before sticking the cellophane back together at the bottom using clear superglue.

The sealed deck is now replaced into the box and the boxes flap is carefully shut so that it is not noticeable that the self-adhesive seal has ever been sliced.

The cellophane cover is then carefully replaced over the box and the bottom flaps of the cellophane stuck back in place using clear superglue.

The other four decks of cards are also prepared in this way and then they are placed inside the plastic bag along with the receipt and you are ready for your arrival at the performance venue.

Incidentally although this sounds very complicated It doesn't take long at all and as only one deck is used for each show, the truth is you need only prepare ONE NEW DECK for each show.

However you will still need to buy Five new decks per show if you want a receipt dated that day for the purchase of five decks of cards which is placed into the carrier bag along with the cards.

EXPLANATION

Quite obviously you know the number or letter on each persons card due to the deck set up which means that you need only glimpse the bottom card left on the deck after the cards have been handed out and you can then reveal them as desired.

The deck set up is also how you reveal the suits on five of the cards at the end of the test and the rest is presentation to make it look like an experiment in Belly Button (Navel) Mind Reading!

There are loads of psychological ploys and subtleties, which I use in this routine which if used and presented correctly will amaze even the most experienced magical performers.

Starting from the top, the first thing is that the moment you arrive at the venue you give the venue manager the plastic bag containing the five prepared decks of cards and ask him to bring them up to you on stage when requested to during the show.

When he is requested to bring them to the stage you ask him to answer a few questions loudly and clearly with a simple yes or no answer.

"You got this bag and the playing cards I need for this experiment before today's show started didn't you?" (He will answer YES)

"And you've been guarding the bag and its contents safely for me from the moment you got them until you walked onto this stage a few moments ago haven't' you?" (Again this is true so answer will be YES)

"Have you kept the receipt for the purchase of these cards for me as well?" (You told him to keep it safe in the bag so again his answer will be YES)

"And finally I've been unable to get near these cards whilst they have been in your possession haven't I?" (You haven't been able so he will answer YES)

"Now before you return to the audience could you just place the bag containing the cards onto that chair there so its nowhere near me and I can't touch them!"

"And finally I've not bribed you, set anything up with you or done anything strange which might affect this experiment have I?" (Again He'll answer no as you've asked for simple Yes/No answers)

The venue manager can then leave the stage and thanks to the way he will have had to answer these carefully worded questions the audience will now be convinced that he the venue manager bought the cards for you and brought them to the venue with him. This means the audience is convinced that you have never been near or touched the cards either during the routine or before the show!

Next you pick up the large foam ball, stand with your back to the audience and toss the ball over your shoulder into them.

The audience are told this was a random method of selecting someone to be their representative on stage and the person who caught the ball or is nearest to it is asked to come onto the stage.

They confirm that you have NEVER met them before and nothing has been set up, then they are told to remove the receipt from the bag and place it in their pocket so it does not get in the way.

They are then asked to remove all five decks from the bag so that the audience can see there really are five different decks before replacing them into the carrier bag.

You tell them to hold the bag by just one of its handles in one hand, to shake up the cards so as to mix up the boxes and then to close their eyes, reach into the bag and remove one deck which will be used for the next experiment.

They are then told to remove the deck from its box and the audience witnesses them tearing off the cellophane from the box, removing the cards from within and them removing the cellophane from the cards.

This further concrete's into the audiences mind that you have in no way ever been near and/or tampered with these cards which they perceive were purchased by the venue manager and never set eyes upon by you until this time!

You then tell the volunteer to face the deck towards themselves and to remove the Jokers and Extra jokers from the deck.

They are told to face the cards towards themselves so that the audience does not get to glimpse that the deck is set up as they are removing the Jokers.

As for the on stage volunteer they will be so nervous on stage and so busy doing as you say that they won't even notice anything strange about the order in which the deck is in.

However the mere fact the on stage volunteer has removed the Jokers from the deck and once again you have gone no where near the pack acts as an even bigger convincer for the audience.

The on stage volunteer can now cut the deck of cards to mix them up as much as they want. As we magicians already know cutting a deck of cards does NOT ALTER the deck set up which will still be in order.

However once again the audience's perception, which will be that the cards have been mixed, makes things seem even more like test conditions.

The on stage volunteer is then asked to give the cards they are holding to any member of the front row of the audience of their choice.

The fact they have a GENUINE free choice makes things seem even more random and unprepared as indeed they would be were it a genuine case of Psychic Powers at work!

As the cards are handed to the person in the front row you say "Could the person who has just been handed the cards please cut the cards and complete the cuts as many times as you want and then give them back to the person who gave you them!"

The original spectator is now told to start on the left hand side of the audience and working from left to right whilst your back is turned give from the top of the deck a card to each of ten different people.

They are told to return to the stage when this has been done and the people about to receive cards are told to look at their cards and just think of the number or letter on them as to think of the suit as well would be far too difficult and time consuming under these test conditions.

A statement such as this concrete's further into the audiences mind the idea that this is test conditions and also the idea that this is a very difficult experiment and that just revealing the letter or number will be impressive enough.

This means that the reaction you will get when you later reveal suits of cards as well will be way out of proportion with what you have actually done!

You now take the remainder of the cards from the onstage person and place them casually into your pocket as you glimpse the bottom card (face card) of the deck remembering what it is.

The on stage volunteer is now returned to the audience to a round of applause and you briefly recap on what has just happened before the revelations begin.

Here the technique of saying what they, the audience perceived (thought happened) back to them instead of what actually did happen is used. Because they think what you recap and remind them of actually happened they will believe it to be fact and this concrete's incorrect information into their minds as 100% truth.

You say something such as "Before I arrived here today the theatre manager went shopping and purchased five new decks of cards." (This is a lie)

"Tonight for the first time on this stage the theatre manager brought the cards to me and confirmed that I had at no time been anywhere near them since he bought them!" (Another lie)

"A volunteer was chosen at random by a ball thrown over my shoulder and they have acted as your eyes and ears at close quarters to me on this stage."

"Your group representative freely choose one of the five decks which have NEVER been touched by me at any point before or during this experiment and then removed them from their wrappings and box before removing the Jokers!" (Some more lies mixed with truth)

"The cards were then shuffled (this is a lie) and thoroughly mixed up by both the on stage volunteer and another person that I have never met from the audience." (Another lie)

"Ten people whom I have never met or prearranged anything with were then each freely given a card from anywhere in the deck and now its time to try the impossible thanks to the power of Navel Mind Reading"

You do your Navel Mind Reading patter and get the people with cards to reveal their Belly Buttons before starting to project the letter/number of their card to you through their base Chakra point by way of a Blue neon beam of light!

From now on its all Patter and presentation which makes this routine so impressive, as the cards were handed out from left to right you know that the stacked deck order will be correct from left to right.

You've already remembered what the bottom (face) card of the deck was when you were given it back and this tells you instantly what the first persons card and each card thereafter will be.

For example if the face card was the Ten of Clubs then the next card in the stack which is the card the first person will have will be the Two of Hearts.

(Refer to the two Mnemonics you learnt earlier and you'll see how easy this information is to work out in just a second or two!)

You can now have all ten people stand up and for visual impact have each person sit down as you correctly reveal the letters or numbers on their cards!

Personally I like to get the 3rd Persons card wrong so that they have to stay stood up and also I then get card number nine wrong as well so that they have to stay stood up as well.

For some strange reason it seems more like a genuine Psychic test if you get something wrong as only a magician would get everything right all the time is the way an audience will think.

At this point you have got eight cards right and two cards numbers or letters wrong and so you still have two people stood up.

You ask the people with a card directly either side of person A to stand up also (that will be the people with the 2nd and fourth cards respectively) and then ask the person stood to the left of person B to stand up (this will be person with card number eight).

You now tell the three people who have just stood up to think of the suit of their card and project it to you as they did before through their Naval for the letter/number.

You tell the two people who's numbers/letters you got wrong before to transmit their whole card both the number or letter and the suit to you.

You then reveal the three suits on the cards of the three people who you previously had already revealed the letter/numbers for, and as you get each one right you ask them to sit down to a round of applause from the audience for projecting the image so well to you.

The routine ends with you revealing the correct identity of the final two cards, e.g. both the Suit and letter/number. This is milked at this point as being the most difficult thing of all to get both images at once especially as you got them both wrong before!

This ensures you thunderous applause when you get them both correct and so ends an amazing yet incredibly easy to do routine.

Re-read what I've said and the way this routine is done and you'll realise just how impressive this does appear to lay people.

Many of the ploys and psychological methods used to make this routine so strong and effective can easily be adapted and used to make other routines you may perform much stronger then they are now – so get thinking!

THE RECEIPT TEST

This is the perfect follow up to "The Base Chakra Projects the Answer" routine and indeed once that routine has finished this one is already set up and its all just down to presentation.

As you may recall the volunteer who came on stage to assist early on in that routine was told to remove the receipt for the cards which were purchased that day by the theatre manager from the bag and put it into his pocket out of the way.

This means that this person now has that receipt in their pocket and you have already done all preparation necessary for this routine.

Before the show get a large sketch pad and using a pencil prepare each page of it as follows using the information which is usually printed onto receipts from large stores:

01) Onto page one put the stores name.

02) On this page put the store managers name.

03) On this page put a three line sum, the top line is the amount apparently handed over by the theatre manager to buy the cards, the second line is the amount the cards cost and the final line which is the answer is what change they got.

04) On this page put the stores VAT/SALES TAX registration number.

The pencil notes made lightly on the pad will not be visible to the audience and act as your cue of what to write down when it comes to performance time!

EFFECT

A spectator is asked if they have any shop receipts on them and then holds one in front of them whilst revealing their Navel ready for projecting thoughts to you on the stage!

Firstly you ask them to think of the store name, you write something down on a pad with a marker pen and then ask the volunteer what name they were projecting, the pad is turned around and your prediction seen to be correct.

Secondly you ask them to project the store manager's name and once again you have written it down correctly onto the pad before they say it out loud.

Thirdly they project the amount spent on that transaction, the amount tendered and the amount given in change and sure enough you have all three pieces of information correct on your pad before they have said them out loud!

Then as a stunning climax you get them to project the VAT or SALES TAX registration number and you also get this 100% correct on the pad before they shout it out loud which WILL lead to thunderous applause.

EXPLANATION

The secret is simply that as the receipt was yours before the show started you have already had access to all the information printed upon it, and indeed have already made pencil notes of this on the pad prior to the show.

Its just down to presentation then to have them project each piece of information as you write it down in clear black marker pen in big letters on the large art pad, before revealing that your reception of the things they are projecting is 100% Correct.

The reason this is so impressive is quite simply because the audience BELIEVE that you have NEVER seen the receipt that is being used.

Those few people perceptive enough to realise that you use the same person for this routine as the one you got up to assist in the last experiment will still believe that you have never seen the receipt.

This is simply because of the belief they have now that the theatre manager bought the playing cards for you and you never made contact with them prior to the show!

However as I have found the MAJORITY of people will not even realise it is the same person, especially as you allow him to stay seated in the audience whilst this experiment is conducted and just get him to shout out information as necessary.

Obviously the longer the delay is between the end of the "Base Chakra Projects the Answer" routine and this one being done, the more likely it is that the audience will not even realise that the same person is being used.

And if they don't realise it's the same person they won't ever think about where the receipt came from, which matters little anyway as those who do make the connection will still be very impressed as their memories tell them you have NEVER seen the receipt!

Just ensure that before the person is asked to project information to you these few questions are asked of them:

01) "Like many of us I always leave lots of rubbish in my jacket, do you have any shop receipts in your pocket?" (They will say YES because they put it their whilst on stage earlier!)

02) "Now we have not prearranged anything before or during this evenings show have we?" (They will say NO)

03) "And to the best of your knowledge & beliefs I have NEVER seen the receipt which you now hold in your hand or the information on it have I?" (They will answer NO as they believe it belonged to the theatre manager and that you never did see it!)

Not only will the audience be amazed as you get each piece of information almost 100% correct but also the person who is transmitting the information to you will be amazed also.

The reason I say almost correct is because to get everything right would seem like a trick, but to get some of the numbers slightly wrong or spelling a name incorrectly but meaning the

Same thing adds a level of realism and enchantment to it all!

I love this routine because like everything I do its simple and allows me to concentrate on the presentation, which with Mental Magic and all things of a Psychic nature is what turns a simple little experiment into a life changing MIRACLE from an audiences perspective!

This is a true REPUTATION MAKER and in my personal experience draws an audience reaction far greater than many so called finger flinging complicated miracles receive.

CHAPTER SIX

SOME ADDITIONAL THOUGHTS ON NAVELS

The Human Navel, which prior to birth is connected to the umbilical cord inside the mother's womb, provides us with our life force before our eventual appearance into this world.

This fact combined with the very believable sounding patter contained within this manual makes the whole concept of Navel reading very credible indeed.

Navel Reading wise I honestly believe that there is more than enough information in this manual to enable you to start giving readings right away.

What's more use the Cold Reading techniques I've detailed within these pages correctly and you can instantly do Palmistry, Tarot and ALL OTHER FORMS of Psychic divination as when all is said and done the common secret is COLD READING!

Should you wish to push the idea of Navel Healing right to the edge then may I suggest that you read the book "Faith Healers" by James Randi which although intended by James to be an expose also happens to be the best "how to" manual on Psychic healing that I've ever read.

Navel Mind Reading wise, with a little imagination almost any Mentalism routine can be used as a demonstration of Navel Mind Reading.

My only suggestion would be that as few props as possible are used as after all you're meant to be a genuine Psychic. Should any props be used they should have a logical reason for being used.

For example with the "Psychic Proverb" test things are logically written down so that there is a tangible object to try and match up with its owner by way of the Navel.

And in the "Base Chakra Projects the Answer" test the cards are merely used as random ways of generating numbers and letters and then later suit symbols for the audience members to project to you by way of their Base Chakra energy point.

These secrets have been earning me a good living, an excellent reputation and extensive regular feature publicity on National TV & Radio shows along with numerous Newspaper and Magazine features – do things right and they will for you to!

CHAPTER SEVEN

FINAL THOUGHTS & COMMENTS ON NAVEL – READING

Despite the fact that I have confessed that now and again I will use elements of Cold Reading when giving Navel – Readings I cannot stress enough that you should also trust your intuition and say what feels like it is the first thing that pops into your head, you'll amaze not only those you are reading for but also yourself at the number of times these things will turn out to be truly accurate.

And always remember to be Positive in what you tell people so as to give them Positivity & Optimism for their future, after all Positive Thinking leads to Positive Actions and Positive Actions lead to Positive Results.

Where possible find out the persons Star Sign before you do the Belly Button Reading and then you can use the simple technique that follows to make your readings even more detailed and accurate:

E-Z WAY TO ASTROLOGY

By far the easiest way to learn to do Astrological readings of people is as follows:

01) Write down each of the twelve star signs.

02) Next to these write down to each of the twelve signs the name of a family member or close friend or at worst work colleague who has that particular starsign.

03) Remember which person relates to which starsign and vice versa and then your job of learning basic Astrology is done!

When you are doing readings and find out what the persons starsign is, you quite simply recall which friend or family member you know has that same star sign and then proceed to reel off information about them.

In otherwords as you know your friend or family member inside out, their personality, their bad habits, and their likes/dislikes etc and they have the SAME STARSIGN as the person now sat in front of you, they should therefore have much in common!

I've been using this simple technique for years and have found through personal experience that by describing the character traits, personality, likes/dislikes and bad habits etc of the person you know well with the same sign as your client you will be 99% correct almost 100% of the time!

Obviously you reveal this information to the client sat in front of you as if it is your expertise of Astrology that leads you to say this about them and certainly you do not mention the connection to family/friends!

Learn Astrology this way and you'll be giving simple starsign readings in less than an hour!

Summing Up & Rseources For Navel Gazing

If you take a few minutes to do a simple Google Search on "Navel Gazing Meditation" you'll soon learn that for hundreds of years many have believed that the Belly Button is the Centre and most important aspect of us as human beings.

You'll also easily find simple guides on how to use your Navel for Meditation and Relaxation.

Finally Here is a link to an article the Sunday People did about me in their print edition back in 1996:

http://www.highbeam.com/doc/1G1-61154404.html

Psychic David Williams has more than his finger on the pulse when it comes to predicting the future.

Given half a chance he'll have his finger in your belly button!

What began as a challenge among friends has turned into a major earner for David, who has read the celebrity belly buttons of boxer Frank Bruno, telly presenter Zoe Ball and comedian Rory Bremner.

And his bizarre technique, based on ancient American Indian teaching, is proving eerily accurate.

"When I did Zoe Ball I told her she'd just moved house, was thinking of buying a car and was having relationship trouble," said David, 21, of Telford, Shropshire.

"I don't know who was me or her, because it was all true!"

He discovered the ancient art while reading text books on fortune-telling.

"The American Indians believed the navel was one of seven energy points which could be used for tapping into a person's psyche.

"By touching someone's belly button I can tell their personality and predict their future," he said.

David claims he can even heal by touching a person's navel. "I was on a German TV show and one of the cameramen was suffering from tennis elbow and had his arm in a sling.

"I held a quartz crystal to his belly button and concentrated on channelling warmth into his body.

"He'd been unable to even lift his arm out of the sling before but when I finished he was moving his arm quite freely," he said.

David, who will be appearing on BBC and ITV in the autumn, is still perfecting his technique.

"I never expected it to take off the way it has but it's getting bigger all the time!" he said.

He's a star turn in People tum test...

The People challenged David to read the belly buttons of six stars. We showed him pictures of their navels but didn't tell him who they belonged to. This is what he said...

MADONNA: "She is insecure, emotional and upsets others easily by speaking her mind. She hides her insecurities by being outrageous."

ROBBIE WILLIAMS: "He is in showbiz, knows what he wants but takes his time to make a decision about his future. He has women swarming all over him."

PRINCESS DIANA: "She's very stressed and worried. She worries about worrying which may have led to psychological problems."

JEREMY BEADLE: "This man has an analytical and serious nature though his public persona is one of mirth. He has a devious streak."

CHER: "She is very loving and caring despite having been hurt very badly in the past. "Despite her suffering she's never let it knock her back and she has reservoirs of confidence and willpower to succeed."

DES O'CONNOR: "This man is always trying to prove himself to others. "He's probably got an inferiority complex and is the butt of a lot of mickey-taking."

JONATHAN ROYLE – BELLY BUTTON VIDEO'S

You may also find these few video clips both interesting and entertaining in relation to the contents of this book:

http://youtu.be/5ismk4VPMy8

http://youtu.be/OHt3JEI-4uU

http://youtu.be/OJR5mUEhhJw

http://youtu.be/c3fgpWQrk8E

Also as my final word for this book I would like to say that I honestly believe that even the most Sincere Psychics and Fortune Tellers use Body Language albeit that most of the time I feel they do so unconsciously with realising so and as such genuinely do think that the information that pops into their head is purely from their Psychic Intuition.

And with regards to Body Language There is one book that I would unreservedly recommend and that is:

"Body Language: It's What You Don't Say That Matters" by Robert Phipps which you can find on Amazon and order from all good book retailers.

From the point of view of developing your GENUINE INTUITON (which I do indeed use as well as the Cold Reading Techniques mentioned earlier) then check out the book:

"So You Want to be Psychic?: Develop Your Hidden Powers" by Billy Roberts.

And last but not least for those wanting to learn more about Cold Reading and How To Duplicate Apparent Genuine Psychic Skills and Talents please check out my massive book:

"Cold Reading & Mentalism For The Psychic Entertainer" by Dr. Jonathan Royle.

Again this is available on Amazon and can also be ordered from all good book stores.

Within its pages I also teach you my approaches of Pawology (Paw and Palm Reading for Dogs), Psychic Tea Bag Readings, Hose Pipe Readings, Pyramid Hat Power, Psychic Tree Slapping and a whole host of other Crazy Sounding stuff which actually is developed from and based on Credible, Genuine and Easily Researched Facts and |Evidence.

I hope you have enjoyed this entertaining and educational insight in the Human Belly button, remember when trying to read your own navel you will have to stand in front of a mirror or get someone to take a picture of it, otherwise leaning over to look at it will knock things out of their usual shape.

You can of course just place your finger into your Navel, Tap into the Base Chakra Energy and take note of the first things that pop into your head.

So yes to sum up, I do believe there is something genuine in Navel Gazing, yes on occasion I have relied on Cold Reading Methods, but in truth the number of predictions that I have made for Celebrities and other people that have then come true and proven incredibly accurate are far too many and too often for me to put them all down to pure co-incidence or guess work.

I however wanted to be totally truthful and honest with you within the pages of this short book.

As Steve Martin the Comedy Actor Says in his character of Jonas Priest in the film "Leap of Faith"

"Maybe what I do is real, Maybe its not, but what's it matter just so long as the job gets done?"

My point on that being if your using Navel gazing to have fun and to entertain then there is nothing wrong with that if it brings a bit of joy and laughter into peoples life's.

And as for Making predictions and such like, only ever state things that are positive and realistic and give people hope and optimism for the future and make them feel better about themselves and in truth you could help that person to be more positive, think more positively and feel better about themselves in life and surely that can only be a good thing?

Happy Navel Gazing

Dr. Jonathan Royle

www.psychicbellybuttonreading.com

www.magicalguru.com

18644456R00060

Printed in Great Britain
by Amazon